Held: Essays in Belonging

HELD

Essays in belonging

Kathryn Nuernberger

SARABANDE BOOKS
Louisville, KY

FIRST EDITION

Publisher's Cataloging-in-Publication Data
(Provided by Cassidy Cataloguing Services, Inc.)
Names: Nuernberger, Kathryn, author.
Title: Held : essays in belonging / Kathryn Nuernberger.
Description: First edition. | Louisville, KY : Sarabande Books, [2025] | Includes bibliographical references.
Identifiers: ISBN: 9781956046472 (paperback) | 9781956046489 (ebook)
Subjects: LCSH: Mutualism--Poetry. | Climatic changes--Poetry. | Belonging (Social psychology)--Poetry. | Symbiosis--Poetry. | LCGFT: Poetry.
Classification: LCC: PS3614.U85 N84 2025 | DDC: 811/.6--dc23

Cover art is "Crocodile and Egyptian Plover" by Sarah Nelson, 2019.
Cover by Sarah Flood-Baumann.
Interior by Adam Robinson.
Printed in the USA on acid-free paper.
Sarabande Books is a nonprofit literary organization.

This project is supported in part by an award from the National Endowment for the Arts. The Kentucky Arts Council, the state arts agency, supports Sarabande Books with state tax dollars and federal funding from the National Endowment for the Arts.

For my dear ones.

Contents

Moss

Back home the sculptor had been carving boulders from huge hunks of Styrofoam that wash up every day on the banks of the East River. Once he screwed together a cairn of three feather-light, super-realistic glacial erratics, which he then tied to the roof of his Nissan. He drove around the city not noticing at first how he shed a pebbly dusting of Styrofoam anywhere he went. Sometimes the first draft of an idea is like that.

A woman at a sidewalk café came over to yell at him as he fed the meter. She had a point, he said, but also, is it more ethical to leave the Styrofoam by the water? Or does it just feel better not to have to know it's there?

We were talking about the aesthetics of salvage in the dining room of a ship chugging its engine across the Arctic Circle, after a day spent walking through a walrus graveyard. The line of skulls and ribs lay at the far end of what had once been a poaching camp where the hunters abandoned anything that wasn't a tusk.

The underside of a sun-bleached flipper bone had grown green with moss. It was the first time I had seen green in weeks. When the sun stops setting, the sky is always gray, the ice and water fall into a range of black, white, blue, and gray. All of the birds and any sea creatures who lifted their heads above the water, it seemed, were black, white, blue, or gray. I didn't know then that just picking up a bone and exposing the moss to the air for the length of minutes it took to get a picture I would later post to Instagram could kill it or cost it years of its slow, slow growth. I didn't realize face down beneath the snow everything that was alive in the bones passes through the moss to become alive again in the thin dust of the rocky soil.

Closer to shore I came upon some green plastic fish netting. I tried to clean up the plastic whenever I encountered it, but a few mossy sprigs had become so entangled with the fraying filaments the two could not be separated.

My offering to the table of artists and scientists were little stories about mutualisms I'd been collecting—wolves and ravens hunting together, figs with calyxes full of their pollinating wasps, crocodiles opening their mouths wide to birds who fly in to pick their teeth clean. I'd gotten some grants to visit deserts and bogs, mixed hardwood forests and tallgrass prairies, and now the Arctic Circle, to observe such creatures living their lives entangled in each other. So that we might learn how to live this way too, I said in the applications, though I wasn't sure I believed my own line of bull.

At the most northern point our ship would reach, the captain dropped anchor and shut off the engines. It was the only time in three weeks we would not be groaning that perpetual roar. An ecologist chronicling the soundscape of narwhals dropped her hydrophone in the water and strained to hear. This was her only chance to catch even a faint echo of their singing and she'd been waiting three weeks for such a moment of perfect quiet. Narwhals cannot bear the sound of ship engines and retreat as far into the ice pack as they can to escape the hum.

The geologist took out a box of ashes we did not know she'd been carrying this whole way. Her brother, who loved the ocean almost as much as he'd loved her, had died unexpectedly the year before and she'd decided to let her part of him go here, in a place he said he'd always dreamed of returning to once more.

We were all silent on deck together for many minutes. Perhaps because this voyage had been delayed for three years due to the pandemic, it seemed as if each of us were carrying a funeral of our own within us. Every face I looked at was somewhere far away. I was too. Then the sculptor took out his guitar and began to play.

I am sorry to tell you the ecologist did not hear any narwhals. She didn't really think she would, she said, and it wasn't necessary to her research. But she was sniffing back what might have been a tear. There are still yet narwhals. There are still polar bears and walruses too, which we saw often enough, specks in our binoculars, but we did not see anything that day except the gray of the sky, the gray of the water, and each other.

H
E
L
D

An Aubade Is a Mourning Song

umbilicate pebblesnail, pyramid slitshell, rubious cave amphipod, heath hen

The acacias shading the Serengeti Plain have hollow thorns. When ants burrow into them, they make a flute of the tree the wind plays as it passes across all those entryways.

shortnose cisco, blackfin cisco, deepwater cisco, phantom shiner, insular cave rat

The scientist in the little Zoom box on my computer screen was explaining to me the symbiotic mutualism between whistling thorn acacias and cocktail ants the same week the last male white rhino died. You might have seen photographs of his colleagues on that preserve cradling Sudan's head in their laps. This man was sitting in a room just down the hall from where those researchers were boxing the last of their data and equipment. He nodded his head in their direction and suddenly they seemed so close. The loss seemed so close.

angled riffleshell, bigleaf scurfpea, great auk, dusky seaside sparrow, silver trout

He brought it up, like he couldn't help it, as people who have just been to a funeral sometimes do, but I didn't ask him what it was like. I remembered eating waffles at the bottom of a mountain with an ornithologist after she showed me two of the last spotted owl fledglings. Once she started crying, it was hard for her to stop.

sea mink, pallid beach mouse, tule shrew, passenger pigeon, brace's emerald

The burrowing of ants into the thorns of the acacia swells them into galls that would kill another tree. But the acacia secretes a nectar from her glands and feeds them. When a large herbivore comes, the tree mimics the signaling pheromones of the ants through her nectaries and the ants attack in a biting and stinging frenzy. Just a few up an elephant's trunk is enough to save the tree.

ainsworth's salamander, maryland darter, green-blossom pearly mussel

And if the elephants and giraffes never come? After a while the tree stops feeding the ants and the ants plunder the rich ichorous sap of the heartwood.

web-footed coqui, thicktail chub, robust burrowing mayfly, stumptooth minnow

I want to believe it is possible to understand each other. The acacia learns to speak ant. The ants learn to answer. Even the scientists find a way to ask how it is in their rough syllables of smokers and sticky traps and short bursts of insecticide.

xerces blue, ash meadows killfish, golden coqui, sloane's urania moth

But without the regular interruptions of the herbivores' dangerous hunger, the ants learn to speak a kind of fear and greed that sounds very human.

acorn pearly mussel, snake river sucker, alabama pigtoe, three-toothed caddisfly

You could say the ants and the tree turn on each other. But another way to understand what happens is grief. Where has she gone, that mother tongue who used to work her way through the leaves, a lullaby that hummed all the way into the roots? How will you live without that melody of a beast grunting a song she's learning from the wind?

bachman's warbler, florida fairy shrimp, amistad gambusia, carolina parakeet

Close

The stalk of goldenrod in my hand is featherweight from the drying of winter, its only heft from a gall orbing the axis of stem three inches down from the blowsy tufts. The gall is a tumorous growth caused by a larva eating just deeply enough into the stem for its saliva to induce this bulbous swelling, about the size of a golf ball, below the browned flowers. *Intima*, the diagram in the botany textbook says, *the inmost coating or membrane of a plant or organ or vein or artery.*

Once purple as a bruise and a little pulpy, but woody this late in the year, I had to saw my scalpel through to the center, where a maggot slept, translucent and curled head to tail. I touched the creature with the tip of my knife to see if it would move and instead it burst a pussy ooze.

Despite how they may seem, the swollen growths and burrowed worms, these galls are not the work of parasites. Invited guests, the larvae feed on a troublesome fungus, the *Botryosphaeria dothidea*, then emerge as flies to pollinate the goldenrod.

The microscope was cool on my eye and I liked how anything I saw seemed to come closer and be further away at the same time. But how I wish I hadn't killed that larva. All he had was being alive and now he is not.

Sometimes I am like the gall, I think, I could hold someone entirely in my arms. Or I could be the maggot, held, the tremble, the twitch. But I know better, or fear I do. I look at my hands and see only the scalpel, the puncture, the tear. I see the sandy bank of the little river where I watched as the kids, laughing, chased each other into the water. And then the way I tried to dive under, but the current kept pulling me back and up. How I could have done everything differently, but what could I have done differently?

And now, at the edge of a field watching another boy, the same age, but who has, oh how I hope he has, his whole life still ahead of him, as he notices for the first time the galls among the goldenrod. I tell him how a wasp comes sometimes and using her ovipositor, which hangs like a spear from the back of her body, she injects her egg, hoping to get near or, even better, straight into the body of the maggot, so her larva can feed on that one.

He's not bored by my botany textbook recitations. He is mesmerized by this wasp and also the ants, with their pincered mouths and acid spit fighting back the beetles that would eat the plant down to her knees. *It's so metal,* he says, and for just a moment I see another child's face glimmer into the world once more.

The wasp is a parasite to the fly but symbiont to the flowers since her young will also grow up to pollinate the goldenrod and keep the fly populations in balance so their galls do not become more than a plant can carry. And then there are the aphids making honeydew from these leaves to feed the ants, the beetles, the chickadees, I go on and on about the goldenrod, tying together its nine worlds. He pulls the galled stalk closer and spots the hole where a winged creature once crawled forth, rested in the sun, and then slowly unfurled those crumpled wings. Behind them, the whole meadow sways each of a thousand million breaths, in, the wind, and out.

Sometimes there is in me the stumped stalk where the ants lose, the beetles chew through the pulp and sap as the whole thing topples. What pollen the fallen flower had is carried on the wind, what seeds sink into the earth, while the flies, the wasps, the ants, scatter.

Sometimes there is just the meadow.

The Owls

On a very bleak day I wrote: "The idea of this book is pointless. A whole lot of carbon driving around looking at trees and thinking about creatures who will soon be dead. Or, like humans, among the survivors, eking out lives in a lonely world, recalibrating expectations to imagine themselves happy in the haze."

I was so sad and afraid we could only get sadder. I did many strange and extreme things in that first year after the accident. Once, in a frenzy of insisting and cajoling, I made my husband, Brian, and our child, Alice, get in the car and ride with me forty minutes out of the city to see fireflies. Because one of these years they will be gone too. Later I took us a thousand miles to the coast to check on starfish, who I'd read were sick and disappearing forever.

On better days I tried to accept change. I wrote essays about how species surge and subside, including us. During the Paleoproterozoic, it was plants who provoked a cataclysmic mass extinction by overwhelming the atmosphere with oxygen.

We reached the H. J. Andrews Experimental Forest after a year when there hadn't been a single spotted owl birth in those woods. So despite having seen a nest, Rita, the ornithologist who let a couple poets follow her into the field, was being careful not to hope.

But there were two baby owls perched on the branch beneath their mother's wings, watching us approach. They'd been working a squirrel carcass, but dropped it in favor of Rita's fresh mouse.

The woods were full of ripe huckleberries we ate as we walked. Rita explained how owl droppings feed the mycorrhizal fungi in the soil that stretch their filaments through the roots to connect all of these redwoods. We jumped across a creek full of caddisfly larvae tucked in the little coiled houses they make out of gravel from the creek bed. So many curlicues shining flecks of quartz back at the sun.

I found this too in an old notebook: "I looked at Alice's teary face and knew for the first time in our lives together I had to make a promise I couldn't keep. 'Everything will be alright,' I said." Even though they were old enough to know a lie when they hear it, to know their best friend couldn't come back the way we want him to, it helped my kid. They slept then, and smiled in the morning. I'd say it again. I will say it again. But the emptiness of my words opened a chasm in me and I have not felt well since.

At the bottom of the mountain we ate waffles in a diner. Adelheid, who was working on a book about disasters, asked if we could talk about grief. She wondered how scientists like Rita, who watch and log every day the way worlds are ending, manage such grief.

Rita said no one had ever asked her a question like that. She seemed grateful for the chance to cry.

In general, therapy has never been as helpful to me as walking in the woods for an hour, but one useful thing the counselor said was that I should try to cry more. She said I should try to cry as often as I could, instead of letting the pain calcify until I couldn't feel at all.

Once I pulled the car over because I saw the body of an owl on the road. Not a spotted owl. Barred, common, smaller than you'd think, softer than you'd think.

There's a way people have of coping by saying it doesn't matter. A logger says to reporters that he doesn't give a shit about any fucking birds when his kids are hungry. But it is terrible to hold the broken body of an owl in your arms, to hold a clear-cut mountain in your view, to fear when you look in your child's face that you no longer have any future to offer them. It hurts and we all know it does, whether we can say it or not. It's not okay and it won't be and how on earth do we live with this terrible ache?

Cairns

I have found it hard at times to pull my mind from the place in the river where the child vanished. For a long time now I wake every morning and sit in the chair where I write and try again to find him. Then I read from Rachel Carson's *The Edge of the Sea*: "The world of inconceivably minute beings, which swim through the liquid film around a grain of sand as fish would swim through the ocean covering the sphere of the earth.... All living, dying, swimming, feeding, breathing, reproducing in a world so small that our human senses cannot grasp its scale."

I had vowed to spend the rest of my life in silence, but that little voice that wants to live began whispering about elegies. I wanted to believe that voice. An ancient Greek metrical form, written in response to the death of a beloved, the elegy mirrors stages of loss—lament, a longing to bring them back somehow, in these words at least, along with fear of how you cannot, and finally, consolation and solace.

As I wrote I began to see once more. The house had become too dim, so I dragged my husband and our child from their corners of grief and drove us across two deserts to the sea, where I knew they would at least wake every morning with the sun on their faces.

Watching Alice picking at mussels in the sand under the shadows of Morro Rock, I thought about the kinds of stories their friends like to hear me tell, about gods and giants and very tiny gnomes who are up to no good. Morro Rock, I might have said, rises out of the bay like a hill or a lonely bluff, the first step of a staircase a god knocked over behind him or the top of a mountain a Titan threw in a fit of rage and grief.

The kids would have rolled their eyes to hear me read from the interpretive signs that Morro Rock is a volcanic plug, a small mountain rising out of the bay, composed of quartz, glass, silica, igneous rock, and partially petrified bird feces. It has been 2.7 million years since all of this was flowing lava. Though they would have perked up when I read the part about how Salinan and Chumash people know this rock as a sacred site on their ancestral homelands. That the Salinan climb it twice a year for solstice ceremonies, while the Chumash consider it too sacred to climb at all. They, like me, like hearing about ways of knowing the land is alive.

On the side facing land, the stones are green with swaying grasses. In the waters below sea otters float, napping on their backs with arms linked together so they don't drift away. The place is a reserve now for peregrine falcons and a nesting site for cormorants and gulls. Less than a century ago, European settlers and their descendants quarried the back half of the rock to build a seawall. You can still see the blast marks.

In this barren and jagged place people build cairns with the hunks of stone that were once also Morro Rock. The whole field from blast site to seawall has become a little cemetery of tiny precarious towers. My child asks why people do this. Such moving and removing of stones is a desecration that upends the worlds of burrowing and microscopic creatures holding increasingly fragile ecosystems together. But here, where the wound is so fresh, tourists like us feel compelled to make their own small mound to join with the others, gazing out to sea, waiting for the wind and waves to somehow make this alright again.

In time the lichens and mosses, the algae from the waves and spray, the bird droppings and creeping of spiders and insects will fill all the gaps between these hard edges. But for now, I put my hand in the star-shaped mouth a person like me once stuffed with dynamite, see the rays of darkened streaks left by the explosion, and feel how this rubble keens.

ARCHIVES AT THE END OF THE WORLD

Word Needed: from the silent depths of winter, a fear you've already heard the last birdsong of your life.

Heidi Quante and Alicia Escott established the Bureau of Linguistical Reality in 2014. A public participatory artwork, they share new words and descriptions of feelings that have no words via their ever-expanding website. They envision an archive to answer the loss for words we feel in the face of mass extinctions, habitat destruction, and climate change. As I read their "dictionary for the future present," I felt the world making a new kind of sense.

Quieseed: an impulse to lay dormant due to a deep intuition not to seed until a fertile environment can be found. A way of knowing emerging from trauma.

NonnaPaura: the simultaneous sensation of a strong urge to have children or grandchildren mixed with an equally strong urge to protect these yet unborn children from a future filled with suffering.

Solastalgia: a form of homesickness one has at home when the environment has been altered to the point of unfamiliarity by climate change. The condition is exacerbated by a sense of powerlessness over the change process.

Chuco헐sol: seeing a brilliant sunset exaggerated by human pollution and knowing you shouldn't enjoy it but nevertheless finding the brilliant colors of the fire intoxicating.

Standing at the iron door to the Global Seed Vault in Longyearbyen, I thought I'd be delighted. This library of seeds carried from every continent to be held in an archive at the end of the world is billed as a collective hope dug into the side of a permafrost mountain. But I could only think instead of the incredible endeavors we manage and the ones we never even seem able to start.

Unsure what to do with myself now that I'd reached the end of a four-thousand-mile pilgrimage to a seed library that only opens its door once a year on a day that was not today, I thought about how we are living inside the unthinkable. Below me, the one dock into this small village on the edge of the Arctic Circle was bustling. Three men in a Zodiac struggled to hold a precariously perched barrel larger than their raft as they crossed the buffeting waves to the cruise ship floating in the deeper waters of the bay. I thought about how much carbon I'd burned to see the glacier hovering over this town. The one my very seeing was melting. I thought about hubris and hypocrisy and my absurd hope that art can change things.

It is difficult to think a way out if you do not have words to describe the state you are in. Quante and Escott give as an example the creation of the word "genocide" in the 1940s by human rights lawyer Raphael Lemkin, who needed a way to name the crimes human eyes could see, but minds could not yet hold.

The Bureau also accepts concepts in search of a word. In the softening soil above the seeds, I made a list of the words I needed.

Word Needed: the gasping beauty of green algae growing in the rocky streams of a melting glacier.

Word Needed: when elders tell of moth blizzards, butterfly swarms, a cacophony of peep frogs so loud you couldn't talk to each other across the porch and you think their memories must be dementia, instead of the time that was.

Word Needed: how good we are at dreaming an eking survival after apocalypses, how few dreams we have to stop them.

All around me arctic avens and poppies lifted their faces to the lightening sky. Hairy lousewort, moss campions, pincushion plants, the tiniest creeping willows stretched out their arms, turning the ice and wind, kittiwake droppings and reindeer slobber, into mountainsides of green for the length of a midnight sun.

Having Had Happened

The more I learn, the harder it becomes to say what is or isn't a mutualism. Pollination is always a mutualism, digestion usually is. All of us are symbiotic with death.

How many seeds on this hillside alone—these early blooming snowboys, for one, the wild ginger for another—are designed with an oily, nutrient-rich pocket that lures the ants, who drag the seeds back to their nests, ensuring they are thoroughly dispersed and buried. Although it hardly makes sense to say "designed." They are themselves, the seeds and the ants, and this is simply what happens.

It happens because it has happened.

Happening, from "hap," as in "to occur by hap," meaning chance, luck, fortune, fate. In Middle English, "fel it hap" means "it happened."

I don't know why things happen or why they don't.

I stood in the middle of an emergency thinking to myself "think harder," as if that would reveal a way out.

It doesn't mean there was no way to save him just because I couldn't think of one.

Sometimes now when I hear a siren, time stops for a while.

The artist and critic Allan Kaprow coined the term "happening" as a way of contending with Jackson Pollock's legacy—it was not really paintings he left behind, but rather that he replaced paint with a new medium: "action."

He described the happening as an "experience that revealed a fundamental split" in consciousness. An "evanescence," he said, the art only exists as itself for a single and fleeting moment, then lingers as a kind of aftermath in the minds of those who were there.

What is sometimes considered the first happening was a performance constructed by Jim Dine called *Car Crash*. In the black-and-white photographs preserved in the archive, there are a lot of cardboard pieces, aluminum foil, and strings of Christmas lights strewn around. The audience caught in the debris wear the faces of people who don't understand what they are seeing.

Happenings are designed to make something happen. In this way they are more like rituals and less like accidents.

I have been trying to invent rituals. To understand, to remember, to bring back, to make whole. They have all come out cringy and try-hard. A good ritual is like a deer path, it begins at first with some amount of intention and need, but keeps becoming as body after body finds the way easier and easier to pass through.

After the accident, after I had failed to think our way out of it, an artist friend went to the river and made a ritual. There was a song, candles, a little boat. She swam in the water and said it was calm and peaceful, said it was hard to understand what had happened there. When the police and EMTs arrived, they said what happened. They tried to explain it.

A lot of what I read about *Car Crash* says the performance was about modernity, technology, and the new medium of photography. But Pollock died in a car crash and, before this show, Jim Dine had almost died in one too. I think after an accident an artist, like anyone else, must learn how to tell a story that can hold the person you were before and the person you were after, the choices you made and the ones you would have made if only you'd known. A story to hold the terror and chance and hap of it all.

Wild ginger flowers don't emit a pungent scent in order to lure pollinating flies to lay eggs beneath the purple bells of their downturned faces. That's just what happens. A smell, a flower, an egg, a little buzzing in your ear, and then this ant dragging a seed three times his size across this hill of fallen leaves.

THE HARD PROBLEM

Here at the edge of winter, the moths are frantic. The snakeroot has just opened its clusters of white flowers, is speaking intimately to the moths that come to pollinate these tufts of blossom.

I am out here in the gray light of morning, on my hands and knees in the backyard weeds, trying to hold a leaf beneath my pocket microscope, because I think maybe there is something I can understand about losing and holding on. The snakeroot is best known for causing milk sickness. People used to die of it all the time and none of the settlers knew it was cows eating snakeroot at the edge of the fields, their poison passing through into the milk. How terrifying it must have been to have no idea why the listlessness came, then the vomiting and trembling. And how terrible to realize later it was such a small and avoidable kind of accident.

Delicate white lines meander all along their leaves. Between poison and poison, microscopic leaf miners live in the skin of a snakeroot leaf, eating a fragile line wending its curves across the veins.

Sometimes people say everything happens for a reason, which I can't believe. But everything that happens does make something else happen, whether I believe it or not.

Soon it will be too cold for the moths to fly.

Like them, the snakeroot is a remarkably gentle being. Threads of fungi knit the roots of one plant to the next, forming a colony that shares minerals from the soil and sugars from the sun. Together they are healthy enough to host without difficulty the parasitic leaf miners slurping their paths through the ichorous streams held in the thin world of a leaf.

It's hard to say whether snakeroot considers itself separate, or if they are all one being—the miners, the fungi, the plant, the colony of plants knitted by the fungi together calling down the moths. I want them to be more than just one fragile body. So that no life is ever really lost.

Philosophers call the question of why we feel like ourselves, and not everything, "the hard problem." Even harder still, they say, is "the binding problem," understanding what accounts for sensations of the unity of experience, like the unity of feeling alive or loving someone who was.

When the snakeroot opened its white flowers, I couldn't understand why I was still here. I was not myself anymore and did not want to be.

A cabbage white fluttered among the autumn blossoms and I remembered an old fairy tale I liked to tell the kids about the threads, thinner than spider silk and glassier than dew. Some embroider us to the air, so we don't sink into the earth; others root, so we don't drift away on the mist. Then I'd flail like a loose puppet making my arms and legs tendril an illegible cursive dance. *Like this.*

Memory

The clematis had taken over the brushy edge of the neighborhood park. When it bloomed the white flowers filled the embankment of a little stream running out of a culvert. The bare branches of juniper it clambered over became a scaffolding. Caves, the kids said as they crawled in. Then houses, ships, the RV they would all someday live in without us. One had the idea to climb up the branches and push through into the sky above. He tested the strength of the vines, then stood with all his weight. From a distance it seemed impossible, how nothing but a cloud of flowers held him up.

The Singular Self

I collect a lot of facts because I think they might fit each other and also maybe me to the universe, but my poor dumb brain just can't come up with how.

Like, there is a crater on the moon named Volta and another named Galvani.

Like, Alessandro Volta was drawn to science by a question he had about the way birds hear, while Luigi Galvani theorized animal magnetism flowed from a muscle in the pelvis. In a lab buzzing with machines cranking forth static electricity and stinking of formaldehyde-soaked frogs, Galvani attempted to prove this organ existed and was the source of a vital fluid in animals that governs all movements, a kind of soul. Volta was distracted from his studies of song and sound by what he thought was the incredible stupidity of Galvani's theory. Volta attributed the twitching Galvani observed to the metal wires he used to transmit current into one pair of frog legs after another.

To prove his point, Volta invented the voltaic pile, which we now call a battery, to allow for more controlled experiments. Reason can be so reassuring. And who really wants to connect a lightning rod to a dead animal, then wait for a storm to flash a leg or wing to twitch, just to prove we are alive? By the end of Galvani's life, it looked to the public as if Volta had won the fight and also discovered electricity.

I collect a lot of facts because when I see you and you ask me how things are, I can tell you what I have been learning as a way of confessing the parts I don't otherwise know how to say.

I wish I had a soul. In my pelvis or pituitary gland or wherever the philosophers want to put it. Instead, I have this vision of the air sparking between two men.

After his death, Galvani's nephew, Giovanni Aldini, who was more showman than scientist, wanted to revitalize his uncle's reputation, and make a buck. He began to conduct public displays of the Galvanic theory of animal magnetism. He noted no paradox or hypocrisy or dissonance in using Volta's battery in his displays: First he showed the crowds one twitching frog, then two frogs, the head of a cow with eyes flying open, two heads of cows blinking furiously, the entire body of a cow quivering on the floor, then the head of one decapitated man opening and closing his eyes, followed by the heads of two connected decapitated men blinking almost in unison. When this was no longer enough of a draw, he petitioned public officials for an entire and intact recently executed person he might try to bring back from the dead through the power of animal magnetism.

Turning the pages of Aldini's compendium of narrative descriptions of the experiments, with adjoining illustrations, I note how his tone is scientific, objective, divorced from feeling. Reading this book, it's easy to forget none of it makes any sense.

In London, 1803, a condemned George Foster was accused of murdering his estranged wife and daughter. The evidence is compelling but not beyond a reasonable doubt. Not only because doubt is so reasonable, but also because his confession was extracted under "considerable duress," which was the preferred euphemism in that age for torture.

Upon learning Aldini would attempt to publicly resurrect him after the execution, Foster tried to commit suicide by stabbing himself with a rusty knife. He survived the attempt, but stayed dead of the way agents of the state broke his neck a few hours later. After, Aldini's coursing current rattled his limbs and forced one eye open, but did not revive him. A man in the audience died a few hours later as he walked home from the dissection theater, allegedly due to shock at what he had seen. At what he had asked to see.

I look at the cratered moon and consider that neither Volta nor Galvani figured out the nervous system, whereby everything an animal thinks or feels is carried through our whole body via microscopic lightning strikes. Or they both did. Out here, alone with the dark and silver light, I'm hoping to catch a glimpse of the egrets. Solitary creatures who only flock together at night when they are commencing their migrations, you need the full moon's light to see how they circle and circle to summon each other. Once in the air, they, like most migratory birds, chart their course using the magnetic fields of the earth via a special organ, not in the pelvis, but in the ear, like a hum or a whistle or a song that allows them to feel a direction at the center of so much spinning.

Breaking

With each wave more barnacles clatter onto the sand. They were once so alive, these stones filled with the squish and soft throbs of being. Thin whisps of blood thread through the pulp of their being. They have no true heart, only a sinus that beats blood through the body.

You can know you are alive, the philosopher Ibn-Khaldūn says, if you wonder how it feels to be a stone.

The acorn barnacles begin as larvae with eight pairs of scuttling legs and two horns protruding from mouths they use to burrow into the blubber of a whale that will carry them for the rest of their lives. Here they begin to ooze from their cement glands, piling up a cavern of this new hard-shelled body, side by side, until they become layered like armored plates across the back, the belly, a fin. From a trapdoor in the shell that covers and is their new body, they release feathery cilia to comb the rushing water cascading across the diving beast for bits of food. Hermaphrodites, they release the world's largest penis (relative to body size) from that opening to plunge across the chasms in search of others.

Humpbacks, fighting to mate or claim territory or maybe it is a conversation to them or playing, crash their barnacle shields against each other with symphonic clangs and booms as shattering shells fall down with the waves, even as the leviathans heave their bodies back toward the air to collide once more.

Aristotle says wonder is the sensation of ignorance.

Sometimes I feel and fear I have learned so much I've lost my capacity for wonder.

Wonder, Francis Bacon, the great philosopher of melancholy, agrees, is the sensation of broken knowledge. Implying that to learn more is to wonder less.

If wonder is the sensation of broken knowledge, then as we learn, we break.

Wonder, says R. W. Hepburn in his book *"Wonder" and Other Essays*, can be a response to the scope of the world. I might, he says, "wonder at my own nature as a wondering being. I am part of nature, yet . . ."

If wonder is born of the realization we are alive now in this moment, then it is also the realization that we will not always be.

Wonder, says Immanuel Kant, is the experience of leaving the limitations of your own mind long enough to look back and see those limits clearly. And to shudder at where you are now, beyond your knowing.

Wonder, I think, may be a yearning to be in shared understanding of the world with someone else. Look, I say and draw my beloved closer to see. Behold.

Before it was possible to microchip a migrating goose and follow her to the ends of the earth where she would nest on a bluff overlooking a frozen arctic sea, people said barnacle geese, who seemed to come from nowhere, hatched from barnacles gestating on a driftwood log. There are ancient drawings of geese hanging by their feet from a tree of barnacles, like bats floating on little islands across the ocean.

Only the most professorial of monks locked in their scriptoriums would have believed this. For the rest it is a story about mystery. Where do geese come from? Where do they go? Why has no one, it seems, ever seen a hatchling or an egg?

And beneath it all, the questions someone wouldn't even know how to ask. That there is a whale longer than a day's journey, heavier than all the memories you hold of someone dear clenched tight in a fist, sounding the furthest reaches of the deep and then beyond.

Silence

I see birds all day everywhere I go. I am trying to learn them by name and song. Because I really believe it is possible to understand each other. And because I am afraid it is not.

The irises of a Brewer's blackbird are yellow. When there were no stars, Vikings navigated by ravens. When the Achaean fleet gathered at Aulis they were greeted with a terrible sign: a serpent swallowing eight young sparrows and one adult sparrow.

Trying to know them is a tangle—European blackbirds are a kind of thrush, most closely related to robins. Red-winged blackbirds and yellow-headed blackbirds are in the North American marshbird family with larks and orioles. The black magpie with his flashing white wings got all the diamonds out of Hell; the blue-into-purple bruised black Steller's jay is the one who delivers the devil his grains of sand.

The water in our creek is running a terribly beautiful shade of sky blue through its ditches and culverts. Someone must have dumped—what? aluminum? a concrete slurry?—it's impossible to say without a spectrographic analysis from our state's Department of Natural Resources regional office where it seems no one has answered the phone since two elections back. Who did this must have thought it didn't matter. I wonder what they think does.

Caym is the demon who also is a blackbird. He understands perfectly the songs of birds, the bellowing of oxen, and the drumbeats of waves. He answers questions in burning ashes or coals of fire, is good at settling disputes, knows the future, and gives true accounts of the things to come. I wonder who decided to call him a demon and what they think goodness looks like.

A blackbird in a cage will prevent lightning, but will be pissed and curse your sky in other ways.

We haven't reached the part when the silence never ends. February comes and the red-winged blackbird sings "konk-a-ree." The sparrow's song is "listen to my evening sing-ing-ing." Then replies, "Oh dear me."

If I can learn to understand them perfectly, I keep telling myself, I will know something about what a life is for. Pierre Jaquet-Droz dropped out of seminary so he could devote his years to clockmaking. His serinette is a music box wealthy ladies used to train caged birds to sing what they were told. What a fucking idiot, I keep thinking, even though I try not to. And also, how do I stop winding these clocks?

Thinking Is a Kind of Feeling Humans Sometimes Have

Like a lot of people, I imagine that if I make my telepathic frustration with the politics on the radio strong enough, I can call it activism. And then I am angry at myself for being one more ineffectual, self-satisfied liberal driving down the highway yelling alone in her car.

Like anybody, I like to look at pictures of animals to unclench. Like somebody who wants to be special, I have chosen a particular niche—in my case eighteenth- and nineteenth-century upper-class European engagements with questions of biology and the sensation of wonder.

Philip Henry Gosse peered through the glass of the public aquarium he installed in 1853. At first his ambition was merely to paint the beautiful underwater flower creatures before they putrefied in a day or two. Then he began to wonder how they live. When he observed the alliance, what he called the "strange affair," between the cloak anemone and the hermit crab to whose shell it was affixed, he wanted to know who was in control. Does the crab pull the anemone along, or has the anemone tentacled all the way into the crab's brain?

Once Gosse realized he needed to add algae to the tanks to oxygenate the water, his creatures lasted longer.

It has taken centuries for the idea of mutualism to penetrate the epistemological system we call "the scientific method," an Enlightenment-era invention that is, you may be sorry to hear, symbiotic with the pseudosciences of race and eugenics, the intellectual justifications of a transatlantic slave trade, the machinery of extraction capitalism, and a deep need humans have to believe themselves to be both "good" and "right."

The sea anemones use the tiny spikes of poison that line their tentacles to shock octopuses away from the crab. In return, the crab shares some of its prey.

By the time the collectors of the Victorian aquarium craze Gosse inspired were done with them, the tide pools off the western coast of England were empty. "Profaned," his son wrote in grief. "Vulgarised." A fundamentalist Christian who proposed in his best-selling books that such pools were relics of the Garden of Eden, perhaps even the Garden itself, the elder Gosse found it hard to understand his purpose in this life after that.

I think Philip Henry Gosse was an asshole who wanted to create the kind of future that terrifies me. I think he was the kind of person who will use the name of God to justify anything they want to be true. I think it takes an enormous tolerance of cruelty to, in the name of science, feed a sea anemone a piece of raw beef until it vomits over and over again for the sake of something called data.

Nevertheless, I believe he was sorry for what he made possible.

Nevertheless, he kept an aquarium's worth of royalties in the bank.

Nevertheless, I turn, with wonder, the illustrated pages of his masterpiece, *The Aquarium*, feeling more and more as if it is my own face that has exploded into whorls of tentacles, each prickled up with sensations of temperature, salinity, the speed of the current, the rippling presence of some other creature I might repel with a shock of poison or draw toward what a human might call my eye but is in fact my mouth, stomach, anus, eggs, sperm, esophagus, intestines, all one singular well of my being.

THINGS THAT REPEAT THEMSELVES

This day ends in the kind of holiday where I feel knotted up in remind me again who is the parasite and who the host? Hellbind, strangleweed, beggarweed. A lot of people, no plants, no sky, in a small room where we tell each other how happy we are to be together.

Hairweed, goldthread, devil's guts. A flowerless, leafless parasite of a vine, she transmits chemical signals across the bodies of the plants as she colonizes them. With each plunge of her little leaching knives she whispers the news from one end of herself to the other. How frightening to imagine other beings living through you, how you'd have to hear their voices in your own mind, absorbing you into them. But it happens all the time—gut bacteria, microbes, pregnancy, cancer, the means of production, whatever it is that calls itself a right-to-life movement. I am constantly hearing the echo of something someone once said to me.

Many ritual events are designed to elevate the sensation that being alive in this world doesn't really matter. One way to describe such gatherings, which I read in Catherine Bell's book of theories on ritual while trying to find a way to justify my absence, is that they are performances of a "mute interplay of complex strategies within a field structured by engagements of power." Witch's hair, bindweed, dodder, "the arena for prescribed sequences of repetitive movements of the body that simultaneously constitute the body, the person, and the macro- and micronetworks of power." Someone hands me a box with a green-and-gold bow. I hand back a bag covered in poinsettias and snowflakes. There are rules here—no one will mention the last election or the next. Which means we will not talk about what we fear and who we love. What I really hate is that when we pretend to like each other we call that nice.

Apropos of nothing, my grandmother told me about the four little girls that she knows are hallucinations caused by the atrophy of her optic nerve, but nevertheless are quite real to her. It is strange, they are starting to grow up. The little one who was a baby has begun to crawl and will be walking soon. The eldest is getting to be a troublemaker.

She seems delighted by them, but knows enough about her wing of the nursing home not to say too much. I'm the person in the family who asks to hear more. There is a narrative in the family about the kind of person I am, and asking about your hallucinations fits right into it. My grandmother had four sisters. My grandmother raised four sons. My grandmother had a number of miscarriages and maybe these ghosts are the daughters she longed for. She also has four granddaughters. I ask her does she think these visions mean anything? She said she was sad to learn the girls were not angels sent to keep her company.

For a long time this baneful vine was written off as an evolutionary dead end, a lonely genus among the plant taxonomies, but then phylogenetics revealed pull-down, love vine, hailweed to be a member of the morning glory family. Morning glories are poisonous enough to kill a person, but it is worth noting, they can also become a kind of sweet potato.

My grandmother doesn't always remember who I am. I said, "Kate, Grandma, Kate." And she said, "Oh Kate—she always was a bossy one." Which was not something I was particularly surprised to hear, having been called that by others many times before. I know well this is the word we say when we are too nice to say "bitch," as well as I know what it means when the most polite of my aunts clears her throat with a long stare. But that my grandmother thought of me these ways too had been a secret of hers and I wish she had been allowed to keep it.

This purple flower, this sweet tuber, the truth of what we are separately and together, I hear the news of my circumstances coming back to me, across a great distance. Like a filament of dawn, *Cuscuta reflexa* knits herself across the green field, a circle closed and tightening.

No. 65, THE HUMANS ARE LOST TO MADNESS, CLIMBING AND CLAMORING EACH OTHER AS IF THERE IS SOMETHING TO REACH

In 1796 Francisco Goya, best known for his paintings documenting the executions of political dissidents, began a visual meditation on monsters, reason, and the relation between. He wrote a lot in his diary about the sleep of reason.

In No. 43 owls and bats whirlwind from a man with his head buried in his arms on a table. *El sueño de la razon produce monstruos.*

No. 24, *No hubo remedio*. A mob of horrific faces sneers at the bound person slipping from atop a donkey. "There was no help." No help, no help, no help.

The series, *Los Caprichos*, began in the realm of literary realism with subtle social satire. There are anguished portraits of the condemned and executed, wealthy elites at their banquets.

Later, and in proportion to the degree of lead poisoning Goya was experiencing from his paints, which he often applied to the canvas directly with his fingers, the caprichos become more deranged. Chimeras of birds and bears howl into open graves, an emaciated dog leaps over their anguished forms.

It is difficult to see ourselves from inside ourselves.

Though it doesn't really help, when I wake this way—raging and confused—I read dead philosophers. Unlike Seneca, who claimed anger is a form of madness, Galen said madness is an activity of the soul.

Avicenna said anger heralds the transition from melancholy to mania.

No. 12, a woman hides her face behind a shawl so she doesn't have to see her own hand inside a dead man's mouth. "Out hunting for teeth."

We've known how sensitive the brain is to lead exposure for a long time—Dioscorides wrote in the first century that lead makes the mind give way. Holidays come and I eat turkey with men who cheerfully swap stories about getting sent home from the mines outside Herculaneum, Missouri, on days when their blood tests came in too high. Their bones are thin now, breathing labored, moods erratic. They blame the liberals with their OSHAs and their EPAs for this.

Lead moves through the entire system. Lead pipes corrode and the lead leaches through the water. Lead bullets fragment on impact, beetles and worms eat lead among the rot. It coagulates then in the bellies and blood of birds. The lead dust from the smelter settles on grass and leaves, in the ditches lining the roads out of town.

There are so many reasonable fears. Lead, in the water, in the air, on the grass, in the dirt, is one of them, but perhaps the least of them. When I count my fears, people who like the power they derive from all this shadowed flapping at the corner of my eyes say: Be reasonable. Don't be ridiculous. Don't get hysterical. Let's wait and see what happens.

What will happen has already happened.

Naked men wrestle into the mouth of hell, sirens fill the air with flapping wings, screaming men with beaks force themselves on braying donkeys, goblins drag people into flesh mounds.

Aristotle also contemplated madness. To become angry, he said, "that is easy—but to be angry with the right person and to the right degree and at the right time and for the right purpose and in the right way—that is not within everybody's power and is not easy."

No. 21, three men pull the wings off a howling woman. "How they pluck her." No. 19, maidens smile while they roast a small half man, half pullet on a spit. "All will fall."

Goya's *Caprichos* are filled with sirens, though instead of being women with bodies of eagles, they are businessmen in top hats with the bodies of chickens. The streets are full of people running around on chicken legs. None look up.

HOMESTEADS

I am holding the thin, lantern-shaped seed husks in my hand loosely, careful not to crush them, as my kid hands me another from the grass beneath the tree and another and another. Where a husk has torn open, I peer inside and see the cluster of seeds that make that shushing rattle sound when we shake them. I spend a long time checking the field guides I keep stuffed under the driver's seat of our rusty and rattling RV, trying to find a name for this strange, beautiful tree dropping these delicate origami folds Alice so loves to gather out here in the middle of the Laura Ingalls Wilder campground.

There is no listing for this seed pod in *Trees of Missouri* or *Trees of North America*. I go down many branching paths looking for a name as my child dumps one pocketful after another in one bowl after another. Like Johnny Appleseed, I say, scattering seeds across America. But when apple trees, which are native to the mountains of Syria, grow from seed, they are wild and unpredictable. They can be bitter or sour or blue or purple. Orchards stretched to fill whole valleys, glinting red and yellow orbs like stars flung across the leaves. I can't remember any more if I also told how only grafted trees can be relied upon to produce edible fruit; seed-grown trees like the ones Johnny planted are only good for cider, since any crabapple can be fermented into alcohol.

I hate this Americana shit so much, I think as I look around the circle of RVs, all flying American flags over their lawn chairs, the most strident also waving that black-and-gray flag with the blue line cutting across the center like an even greater threat. I try to remind myself I don't have to be here. I'm the one who said it would be interesting to go home again when Brian took the freelance job writing a travel guide to Missouri. I'm the one who wanted to see if there might be such a thing as home at all.

I'm also the one choosing to keep asking docents, campground hosts, and obsessively knowledgeable fans why Laura Ingalls Wilder thought it would be so lucrative to move to Mansfield, Missouri, in the 1890s when her heart seems to have been entirely in the northern plains? It has something to do with shifts in the timber industry, right? Which has something to do with the treaty the US government signed with the Osage Nation in 1808, the Indian Removal Act of 1830, slavery, the abolition of slavery, Reconstruction, the way Jim Crow replaced Reconstruction?

Of course I know the answers to these questions. I mean, I know how I would answer these questions. What I don't know is what story the people I used to call neighbors, cousins, friends tell themselves. I don't know, but would like to, how they live with it all. Brian says I should ask whatever I like, but try not to get us kicked out until after he has figured out the 168 words he needs for an entry in the book.

Laura was quite good at telling a story people could live with. That's why her farm is bursting with tourists who want to touch even just a table leg of it. Before she became a famous novelist, she wrote a weekly column about the idylls of Ozark farm life, designed to recruit settlers to the region, where they would buy land by taking out loans from Mansfield Farm Loan Association, where she served as secretary-treasurer on the board of directors and from which she derived far more wealth than she ever did from publishing books about her childhood. Any pastoral nostalgia you've ever heard about the old Ozarks is probably some version of a story Laura once wrote for the paper.

Brian is also good at this kind of story, which sometimes impresses and sometimes irritates me. I wish it were possible for him to be as principled as he is charming. He sighs. Do I want him to buy the gas to drive us out of this place or not? I tell him I've been thinking maybe I could write a shadow guide to his, one that tells the truth. He laughs. Good luck selling that.

Sometimes we're testy with each other because there's only so much peace we can make with how I came to him one day and said I couldn't be a farmwife anymore. It's been five years or more now since I signed a lease on a house in the city, but we can only make so much peace with what he gave up, including a farm in the foothills to the Ozark Mountains that had been in his family for five generations. That with it he gave up the certain feeling he once had that he belonged somewhere. All so he could stay with me.

Even when I was a girl I had no use for the *Little House* books teachers and relatives loved to gift. Sure, Laura seemed plucky enough, but one look at Ma's face behind her bonnet and it was easy to see where that fantasy ends. In the memoir of another nineteenth-century girlhood on the plains I like much better for how it tells the truth, Zitkála-Šá recounts how she was taken to the Carlisle Indian boarding school, separated from her language, her culture, her people, her family. Such a young child, hardly older than Laura was in that little house in the big woods, she was goaded onto the train by missionaries who promised her fields of sweet red apples, as many as she could eat. As we walk around Laura's farm, each crunching an apple the docent handed us from the old orchard, I can't stop thinking about the scene in Zitkála-Šá's memoir when, after a great struggle, she is tied to a chair and missionaries cut her braids away. "The first day in the land of apples was a bitter-cold one. . . . And though my spirit tore itself in struggling for its lost freedom, all was useless."

I'm sick of Laura. Laura depresses me, her apples depress me, everything about this place does. Except this strange misbegotten tree. I download a plant ID app to find its name, which is golden rain tree. It is so called for its golden blossoms in spring, which fall like rain and make a glowing pool in the grass. Native to the temperate forests of Asia, in the Japanese tradition the rain tree is planted over the graves of scholars.

I read from Wikipedia on my phone, which gets a couple bars if I hold the machine up to the sun pointing toward the highway, that in China the leaves of the golden rain tree have been used to make a black dye. The seeds become beads. The trees are hardy, good to plant along coastlines or use as windbreaks. Introduced to Europe in 1747, America in 1763; in 1809 Thomas Jefferson received a shipment of seeds from Madame de Tessé, a French aristocrat and botanist with whom he frequently traded plants. In their letters they often share complaints about the difficulty of the Venus flytrap. Jefferson describes to her his vision of filling the fields of Georgia with olive trees, though Jefferson's olive trees never would take root in this continent's soils the way the apple trees did.

Wormley Hughes was one of many enslaved people at Monticello whose work we are really talking about when we say "Jefferson's research" or "Jefferson's innovations." When anyone says "Jefferson" was a great botanist and gardener, they mean Wormley Hughes. Hughes is never mentioned in these letters, but I often wonder what he thought of such grand plans for olive trees and all the rest. Did he have an anti-colonialist critique of non-native species or did he just love to put his hands in the soil and see what he could make grow? I wonder, but know I will not find the answer in any archive or on the lips of any docent, so I say his name and peer at the drawing of him that was found among Jefferson's papers. How young and handsome he looks in his dapper suit and hat and thin mustache.

Around Laura's orchard the path was lined with hot pink pokeberries. Soon they will ripen to a rich purple. As we walked along earlier in the day I rambled about how pokeberry juice mixed with vinegar makes a good ink. My husband and kid weren't listening, had long since lost interest. *Where are you going with this?* Brian asks whenever I read him some of my notes. *It's too many facts, Mom*, Alice groans. I've been told I should try to focus on just one thing and it's true I'm starting to feel like a conspiracy theorist as I stitch the farthest reaches of my people's cruel history into a story about a place I call home.

Jefferson never traveled this far west, nevertheless, his name is on the capital and the sides of buildings everywhere we turn, hanging over hospitals and elementary schools. His shadow fell even on the fields here when he used a recipe for pokeberry ink he learned from the Algonquin people to write the Declaration of Independence, including the line about "the merciless Indian Savages, whose known Rule of Warfare, is an undistinguished Destruction, of all Ages, Sexes and Conditions." And later when he signed his name to purchase all the land west of the Mississippi.

Where I'm going with this is that I had this idea that if I could figure out whether it was Laura or her husband Almanzo, their daughter Rose, or some later neighbor who planted the rain tree, maybe I'd know how I could ever belong.

But that's not how belonging works.

A few days earlier, I'd stood in front of William Clark's desk at Missouri's American Indian Cultural Center in Van Meter State Park. His table piled high with books and turtle shells and sheaves of paper, jars of feathers, pens scattered among it all. How much it looks like the desk I set up for writing each time we park our rig. While Brian connects us to water and electric, I put out my little stack of books and field guides among the jelly jars I've filled with rocks and seeds and very nice felt-tip pens. Surveying Clark's lists of plants and notebooks thick with pressed specimens, it occurred to me I have spent my life trying to avoid the trap of farmwife, only to become a colonizing gentleman instead. William Clark once said if he went to hell for anything it would be for the treaty he negotiated with the Osage in 1808. I think about all I might go to hell for.

One idea about belonging I come across while reading Dionne Brand and Robin Wall Kimmerer, Wendy Makoons Geniusz and Christina Sharpe meditating on the grief of displacement and dispossession is that you belong to a place after you've buried someone there. But their ancestors survived displacement and dispossession while mine, who came to Missouri to open grocery stores and butcher shops and make fine dresses and acquire rental properties, caused and profited from them. Another definition I find is that belonging is the wrong question altogether.

I'm not sure what the right question is, so I ask about the tree instead. Deep in my university library's research databases I come upon an account of US scientists who traveled to Korea to study golden rain trees. They walked all over a particularly remote village rumored to have many great and ancient specimens, but were frustrated after a hard day not to have found even one. They sat down for dinner at an outdoor café and then realized right above their heads was an almost unrecognizably scraggly rain tree casting a thin shadow across the patio where they ate.

Seeing their excited pointing, an old woman came out of the kitchen and told the scientists through hand gestures and their clumsy translations that it had been her family's responsibility to care for that tree for generations. Some decades ago, central authorities claimed the tree's land from their family and forbid their meddling in the tree's or the state's affairs. The tree has not been healthy since, she said. This had happened to all of the trees in that region. The scientists only mention this anecdote as a strange and amusing aside, entirely tangential to the data that would follow. As I read, I wondered at all the knowledge they let pass right over their heads. How many generations of knowing this tree might that old woman have held? Perhaps all of them.

I'm ashamed of how much I love this life on the road that I

know is just the latest iteration of that settler colonialist dream of a ribbon of wagons stretching out to the horizon. I've already begun to plan the application for funding that will allow us to live this way for another year and maybe even another one after that. To wake every morning in some state or national park, a president's name or a governor's planted on signs over native land, beneath a canopy of green. I drink coffee by the embers of last night's fire, loving how Brian and Alice's sleep breathing carries through the open windows, trying not to dwell on how much of Pa there might be in me. Pa, I learn in *Prairie Fires*, a book about Laura Ingalls Wilder I can't find anywhere in the gift shop, left that little house in the big woods to avoid the Union draft and go squat an illegal encroachment on Osage territory, where settlers were gathering for the express aim of creating the political necessity for the US government to break the treaty of 1825. The minute a single Osage person snapped under the pressures of overpopulation and land desecration, constant terror and the grief of settler violence, the government would have its justification for the next wave of genocide. This happened in 1865 and again in 1872. None of this is on any of the signs in the museum.

What is in the museum, lost in the labyrinth of glass cases stuffed with letters, hornbooks, butter churns, awls, and axes, is Pa's fiddle. I stared at it for a long time, all of my critiques and histories and questions and answers silent before the taut strings. There is one scene in *Little House in the Big Woods* I really do love, when Pa plays and everyone jigs joyfully. The crowd calls Pa's mother from the kitchen and she emerges, feigning reluctance, as she wipes her hands on her apron. Fine, she sighs, and begins to stomp her feet. Then they fly. The men try to match her pace, but by the end of the story they have all given up and she dances alone in a circle as they clap and slap their knees and cheer. Every *Little House* book begins someplace new. Each time Pa packs the family into the wagon, they push farther and farther from his mother.

Of all the scenes in all the books that were read aloud to me as I sat criss-cross-applesauce on one grade school carpet after another, it was this little memory Laura has of her grandmother that I liked. It reminded me of my own grandmother, who taught me to dance in her living room, while her sister held a fiddle to her chin long after the bow had begun to tremble in her hand. Even when her hearing was almost gone, the notes so far away she struggled to tune, my great-aunt would sway and tap and bend as she played to see how the littlest kids danced circles around the cheery old songs my grandmother made up words to after she forgot the real ones. If I think very much about Pa's fiddle, I start to cry a little for how much I miss those women.

Brian comes up behind us to admire the mandala of lanterns and sticks and acorns and pebbles our kid has been making in the grass beneath the wide arms of the rain tree. He's chewing on an apple right in my ear. I ask where that came from and he says, "Laura's orchard." He waited until the docents left for the day, then hopped the split rail fence and stole a bag full. They're green and sour, the way he likes them. Thieves upon thieves, I think as we throw our cores in the stand of woods lining the ditchy creek that runs along the road that tomorrow we'll follow out of here.

A Sense of Belonging

There are a lot of good reasons to leave a place and one of them is that you hate everyone there and another is that everyone there hates you. It is terrible good fortune when these occur at the same time.

The ditches at the edge of our field were thick with poke, which I did like, even loved. The poison root grows down deep and snaggled like a mandrake.

Poke will drink cadmium, manganese, whatever heavy metals our fertilizers leave behind. It will drink and it will grow, putting on those berries that bulge weird eyeballs at passersby.

The cowbirds stalk the ditch of the field eating the vitreous purple of such toxic fruit. I had to be so angry to become someone who didn't need to be angry anymore.

I will never belong to another place as I do to those fields of pokeberry, leering first hot pink, then ripening to a mulberry black as the hardiest of birds flutter from one stand to the next, then off into the blue of some idea they had about what sweetness there might be. I couldn't have known then how I'd miss them.

Zugunruhe

A cowbird lives most of her days in the grass, eating flies and gnats kicked up from the dust by grazing livestock, who have replaced the bison, her once-partner in being of the prairie. She survives. She flourishes. The cowbird is one of the creatures who multiply in this wreckage, and out of admiration for that resilience alone, I could watch her forever.

Through my binocular view here at the edge of the field, I track the cowbird tracking birds I cannot see in the dark-green shade of the deepening woods. A warbler maybe or a tit or one of the dozen other suitable hosts flies off for food or a piece of moss and the cowbird dashes in to overtake the empty nest and lay her egg among the stranger's brood. She pushes a little blue one out to make room for her own, large and white with brown speckling.

Then she checks on each of her other eggs scattered throughout the forest. From perches on overhead branches, she counts. Cowbirds practice a brutal form of parasitism. If anyone refuses to host by kicking her egg from their nest, she creeps on the rest while the parents are away and pecks them all into a sopping mess of yolk.

In time her cowbird hatchlings will be cared for by the songbirds, warmed and fed and raised as one of their own among the trees. Which begs many questions, though the most perplexing for biologists are: How do cowbirds know to find each other in the grasses later? How do the females learn the complicated calculus of choosing and parasitizing the perfect nests? Or, another way to ask is, How do the cowbirds even know they are cowbirds?

Such an old question—*How do you know who you are?*—and one I thought I'd outgrown. One I thought I had to outgrow. My kid asked me what gender was one morning while I was brushing my teeth and thinking about what yearning means to a bird. "I mean, what is a woman anyway?" My kid was in the first year of middle school and getting asked every day, "What are you?" Once in science class a boy pointed and said, "You're just a fat cow." My poor kid. The first time someone at school just knew to interrupt and say, "They are Alice"—dear Alice, who didn't yet know terms like gender euphoria, couldn't stop talking about the way it felt to finally be understood.

I told my kid there wasn't as much language for gender available to me when I was young—I thought we just had to make a word like *girl* stretch until its meaning could hold us. *Woman*, to me, is the word for all the sexist bullshit you'll have to put up with. But, the truth is, I don't know who I might have been. It's so common—every girl, every kid—I don't know who any of us might have become.

The current best theory for how cowbirds become themselves is that they feel called to the fields, an inexplicable and compelling desire. Around their twenty-fifth day, just as the young cowbird has begun to fail in their echoes of their fellow nestlings' warbling songs, they are overcome with a kind of yearning. It always happens in the night, they leave the forest in search of a field, looking for a certain shape of flitting shadow among the grasses maybe, or a taste of something beyond memory, their cowbird mother's song in the distance is one hypothesis, a mate is another, I have speculated that they feel something welling up inside which a human might call a sense of purpose.

If you keep the cowbird in captivity, they will never learn to be themself. They will instead try and try and try to learn the song of their hosts. They will spend their life singing so badly such songs to siblings who are confused and misunderstand every note. The cowbird without a field will be alone, stymied, unable to imagine the life their whole body is reaching for.

I have found it impossible to contemplate the extraordinary adolescence of cowbirds and how much they must unlearn to become themselves without also thinking about one particular kiss. There was a streetlight glowing orange over our heads. The sky beyond was the starless purple of an hour about to turn over to morning. I wouldn't have guessed I could become someone who liked to be Frenched across the hood of her car. From another world I heard a group of guys hooting—it was at us, but *so what*, I thought, they are trapped in another moment entirely.

When summer ended, he decided to enroll at my college instead of his. Without telling me, he checked a box to live in my dorm. He never went to his classes, just waited for me to finish mine. And after I broke up with him, he wrote to my friends describing every harsh thing I'd ever said about them in confidence, taking some words out of context, twisting others. To this day I don't always know who got such a letter and who didn't, am not sure why some friends did or did not stop taking my calls, whether it was his words or just me. Then, he dropped out, packed up his car, and drove back home, where he would, every week or so, leave black roses and letters describing our intimacies on my parents' front porch.

Where in God's name does someone go to buy black roses?

You'd have to look that up and probably drive a long way. Or plan ahead to dye and dry them yourself.

There is more, but I hate thinking about it—I still feel so stupid and ashamed. I wish I could tell you I didn't let that ex-boyfriend change me. For years, if you'd asked, I'd say it was fine. I'd say it didn't even matter. For years it didn't even occur to me how common those moves from the abuser's playbook might be—alienate, isolate, intimidate, control. Of course it changed me. My family and my friends, whether and for what they blamed me, that changed me too. I'd never lose myself under a streetlight now.

Lately I have been boring the people dear to me, as I have perhaps been boring you, with all this talk of birds and how they find themselves. I go on about how the kind of calling a bird feels to migrate is so strong German researchers had to invent a word, *zugunruhe*, for it. It is how I tell them too, after a fashion, how afraid and angry I have been. How I have tried to be something else, but ever since I was very young I have been both. How I didn't realize until I saw my child, an age I once was, becoming.

And then I pause to take a drink from my wine and look out at this moonlit field beyond us, where the shadows are flickering through the night and my child, almost but not quite too old now, holds a firefly between cupped palms. A little door opens in my chest, something in there like a bush of red berries, grasses swaying just beyond it, bird calls drifting on the wind. Being a teenager in love in a parking lot is one of the great joys in this life.

There was an exquisite ache I thought I saw in his eyes. But it was not in him, that yearning like a song I was supposed to follow, it never was. It was the gorgeous depths of a night glowing beyond him. It's taken so long to find the grasses growing silver and gleaming from the loamy ash of a brushfire just burned through, stars of thistle blinking from the wallows cattle have rolled and burrowed into the earth.

My child opens their hands and the light blinks back. Let there be no end to this expanse. Let us become common in it, our comings, our goings, our songs or squawks or whatever it is we are, calling, roaming, following a feeling we don't have a word for.

The Complex Biological Entity Known as Sky

Ægir was a poet and the only mortal to ever enter the house of the gods. He devoted his life to the study of dark magic just to find a way in, and once there all he did was ask the gods about words. How, for example, should one refer to the sky?

Bragi, the god of poetry, instructed him to say: Ymir's head, the giant's skull, the burden or heavy load on dwarves, the land of the sun, the land of the moon, the land of constellations, or the house of the air.

Ægir was perhaps in search of a way to know what to say and what to do to make his world more blooming and thick with birdsong. Or perhaps he feared his own vulnerability to psychological mechanisms like confirmation bias or ego protection. Or maybe he wondered whether he needed more words to make more sense, or less for it all to make less. His questions are recorded in the *Skáldskaparmál*, also called *The Language of Poetry*, the second and very boring part of that great Norse epic, which opens with the story of the world tree, the Valkyries, Loki, Thor, the hammer, Valhalla, and the inevitable destruction of the nine worlds.

Norse poetry is characterized by its use of kenning, ambiguous or roundabout figures of speech that replace ordinary nouns with a series of descriptive words knitted together by hyphens. Battles are spear-dins, fire a bane-of-wood, wives are girls-of-the-house, a serpent is a valley-trout, a ship is a sea-steed, gold is called serpent's-lair or Sif's-hair or Kraki's-seed. It is also a poetry that has been claimed and co-opted by a great many white supremacist movements, despite how kennings are an exercise in imagining how you would see the world if you had lived your life in some other body—that of a tree or a god or a planet or a snake in the grass—any body other than your own.

Scientists thought it would take millennia to heal, but when the sky passed over the burn wound at Mount Saint Helens, a cascade of aeroplankton dropped onto that crater and became the beginning of the next forest.

Sometimes I feel like a spider who has thrown myself into the air via the silk of a kite that is a part of and made from me. Sometimes the haze stretches halfway across the continent, from where my friend is driving her car of kids, the cat, important papers, bottles of water, a box of family photographs, whatever would fit in the suitcases, down the burning mountain, to me at this desk, trying to create a path between my life and that of an aeroplankton. Like, I am so small I paddle my wings through the gas particles. As if they are liquid to me. As if there is no such thing as liquid vs. gas to me.

Many mornings I pass a shortcut through the Department of Chemistry, to get out of the snow or rain on the way to my office in the Department of Co-Opted Radicals. An R1 university runs on funding from the Department of Defense, DuPont, Bayer, 3M, whatever they decide to dump in our water and burn into our air. Every morning I walk near the offices of the leading experts on cloud seeding. From this place of so much security I look out the windows at the drizzle we may, peer review willing, come to know as the breaking blue of someone else's drought.

The *Skáldskaparmál* is boring to read, but I love it because the name for a being matters and all the beings in *The Language of Poetry* are named in relation to something else. The sea is the whale-road, a boat is a wave-pig, a raven is called swan-of-blood, the sun called glory-of-the-elves, the wind is breaker-of-the-trees. We are ourselves, but we are not only ourselves.

Georgia O'Keeffe, another great poet of the sky and clouds, once wrote in a love letter, "It is absurd the way I love this country ... I am loving the plains more than ever it seems—and the SKY—Anita you have never seen SKY—it is wonderful."

I wake in the middle of the night repeating, they said, I said, trying to understand how it is to be someone else. How another way to understand the sky is as a complex biological entity composed of microbes, viruses, bacteria, approximately forty thousand species of fungi, protists, algae, mosses, liverworts, also spiders and aphids, all living out significant portions of their life cycles on the wind. Researchers are interested in how the use of certain compounds might encourage sudden exponential growth or death of bacteria, perhaps a more effective and reliable method for shaping the weather than the current practice of cloud seeding with silver iodide, which is as capricious as the weather itself. Don't they know the name for war is weather-of-weapons? That a sword is blood-worm, icicle-of-blood, or wound-hoe?

The scientists I've talked to are largely nonplussed by cloud seeding. They shrug and say it's only salt and barely works. They laugh-sigh at the conspiracy theories coming from the congressional representative that the president could conjure a hurricane. But my government signed a treaty in 1978 banning the use of weather modification for hostile purposes. Having seen what my government does with its treaties, I despair the sky might become venture capitalists' newest commodities market. Already I miss the stars we can no longer see through the relentless glow of our light upon light. I miss the blue slipping away into the gray haze of globalized industrialization. When I fly across this continent I look at the window for hours, watching how the square of one farm field stitches to the next, waiting but never seeing more than a thin thread of wild green here and there, tracing the edge of a creek.

The sky is an ethereal and transcendent blue. Though sometimes I look up and it seems the only name she has is What-the-fuck-is-wrong-with-you-people? But she is Where-our-minds-go, she is House-of-our-breathing, she is Mother-of-water, she is Forever-in-a-day.

Nowhere Else

Driving the long stretch through lava fields, large blankets of pink and magenta flowers stretching up the mountainside caught my eye. As I pulled the car over, my kid in the backseat groaned, my husband groaned, my mother-in-law said, "Oh you two, leave her alone."

I step into a ditch to see more clearly that these are hundreds of pink spikes of flowers rising from a bed of red leaves and stems that hold each swaying face to the rest of herself. I peer at one thumbnail of a blossom and then at pictures in my field guide. A kind of knotweed. They were growing from the crevices between rocks shining silver with lichens. Every stone was so jagged it was hard to walk—the wind and the rain and the lichens and weeds had hardly begun the work they would do to soften this place to soil again.

I was preoccupied on that drive with ideas about the everyday workings of colonialism and how the left hand doesn't always know what the right is doing. And all that the ease of such ignorance, or the pretense to such ignorance, enables. On the left side of the highway was a military base. While my family played I Spy, I counted how many armored trucks passed us.

On our right were the Mauna Kea observatories, where scientists trained in western epistemologies will tell you they are engaged in a beautiful endeavor trying to see the past and the future through spots of distant light. The thousand or more Native Hawaiian protestors and allies, who for months had blocked the access road to these telescopes, had retreated down the mountain in the face of what seemed like a toothless compromise and the overwhelming threat of police brutality. What remained was a single tent, empty that day, posters with protest slogans hanging from the fencing around the parking lot, and a series of large informative signs explaining this mountain is a sacred place, home to the gods who sustain the mountain and the people. And that development of another telescope, like the ones before, would pollute and destabilize the fragile aquifers that nourish this land.

The sky was so clear we could see snow gleaming at the top of the mountain. And through that snow, the off-white domes of the six observatories already in place. Traditionally, land in Hawaii was parceled out not in the rectangles typical of European allotments but in triangles that trace up the side of the mountain and down to the sea. Because fresh water collects at higher elevations and trickles down, the triangle ensures people have to think about the wellbeing of the entire watershed. There is no upriver to fight over and no downriver to disregard. The very highest elevations were the homes of the gods—you needed permission and a very good reason to go there. To take so much as a tree from that precarious and ethereal place required a major sacrifice.

Funding for astrophysics often comes from the Department of Defense, planning for the next war, or from private industry, allocating their venture capital according to predictions about future profits in sectors like satellite surveillance. A public university funded my trip here too, so I could write poems about how I feel about lava crickets. My left hand thinks it is hacking the system for the sake of art and conservation, while my right knows it is convenient to send the intelligentsia on colonialist field trips to write ineffectual and inward-looking poetries.

Pink knotweed is known as one of the prostrate herbs. A naturalized non-native species, it kneels at the foot of Mauna Kea. The alpine summit is Wao Akua, the realm of the gods. It is a sacred place. I did not go there, as I had no need, no invitation, no gift or sacrifice. I stood with the lovely knotweeds, among what seemed that day like the remains of the protest, a quiet before the hum of bulldozers began again. I could not see then the ingenuity of activists and their lawyers regrouping in living rooms in the neighborhoods below. I could not imagine then anyone saving anything. But it has been five years since that day and no construction has resumed.

The summit was formed in an ice age when the lava was frozen. Even now the aeolian ecosystem freezes nightly, the ground is a layer of ashy permafrost, there is intense ultraviolet radiation at such heights. It is home to agrotis moths, cutworm caterpillars, lycoṣa wolf spiders, springtails, the wēkiu bug. On an island overwhelmed by invasive species witnessing one extinction after another, these acres are a last refuge.

The palila, a lovely yellow-headed member of the honeycreeper bird family, now lives on this summit and this summit alone, eating the māmane drifting down from passing clouds and fluttering among the hardiest shrubs of ʻōhiʻa lehua, which put forth incandescent blooms of pink, each one opening like a radiant sun in the distance.

A Green Bejewelment

You will know the ash trees by how their deep brown bark is faded to a pallor of honey and cracking in rectangular chips that fall to the snow. Everywhere along the trunk are little explosions bursting out from the xylem. These are the signs of an emerald ash borer infestation, and nearly every tree in this floodplain has them. It is a pandemic with a high rate of mortality.

I walk this path every morning. My species too is experiencing a devastating pandemic. I put my finger on the path a larva once made and trace the cursive wood it chewed its winding season through. Their paths look like smaller versions of the meander scrolls the river has made of this place as it bends away from, then around, then back again toward its old embankments.

The Meliae, the nymphs of ash trees, formed when the first drops of blood fell on the earth. That I am here telling this old settler story of trees is one of the signs that first violence has never ended.

The ash forests near me are healthiest where traditional Potawatomi basket makers harvest trees regularly. Removing some canopy cover lets in enough light for the next generation. One way to interpret this is to say trees and people need each other.

At the base of the great ash tree that holds the worlds together you will find the three Norns, fates who pour fresh water on the roots every morning and polish the trunk to protect it from disease. Over their heads four stags leap through the leaves. Only after they have cared for their tree do the three turn to their other work, deciding each day who lives, who dies, who flourishes, who suffers, how long.

I love this story, but also hate it as I learn more, and then more still, what my cousin thinks the tattoo of Thor's hammer across his chest might mean. Sometimes I'm so angry at what my people have made of everything down to our mythic memory of a sacred tree rooted in the place we come from that I think I could pull that ink from his skin with my bare hands. But then I remember anger can be just another way to avoid looking inward.

I know I do not understand this place where I live, I know I am only trying.

All of the scientific literature uses the term "invasive species," though I try not to, because words create our reality as much as they describe it. Last week a white man in Atlanta murdered eight people, six of them Asian women, and another dislocated a woman's jaw after yelling slurs I won't repeat here.

In their home ecosystems, in the expansive forests of the Taroko Gorge, from where they were carried one logged tree at a time, these beetle populations were controlled by a wasp that punctures their eggs and devours their larvae. This year there have been signs that this wasp has at last arrived in North America too. Which may help establish a balance that benefits the trees, though there will surely be other unforeseen ecological consequences to add to the cascade of colonialism's consequences.

I took a vow, as scientists also do, not to use metaphor to describe other beings. My friend, the staunch post-structuralist, said this would be impossible as language itself is a metaphor. I said failure was part of the point. He said he would think about that, but died alone in his apartment in that year of pandemic lockdowns before he had a chance to reply.

Once I told him I could empathize with something I thought he was feeling and he said the very idea of empathy was offensive. One of the ways the British government justified the colonization of Sri Lanka, the place where he was born and fought, survived and grieved, was by "proving scientifically" that the Sri Lankan people were not capable of empathy.

Of metaphor generally I do not know what he might have come to think, but he brought me to easy agreement that empathy is a dangerous form of comparison that erases even as it pretends to relate.

More difficult to explain without the illusion of empathy is this sensation that I do not always know where my thoughts end and another's begin. When I touch the trunk of an ash and bark falls away from my hand, I try to feel something of the tree. But all I can find is myself, the way my breath moves down my arm, to my hand, and then the hum of grubs thrumming their feeding bodies through the cambium and further up through me.

First one tree is failing, then a forest of them, and then the beetles too cannot live inside the waste of their own ravenous hunger. Probably a beetle cannot see its place in the world clearly enough to miss, to long for, to love the wasp it evolved alongside.

And the beetles are beautiful. This too is important. The iridescent gleamings of their bodies are like oil-slicked rainbows—a droplet pooled on each leaf.

My friend asked me to meet him for a drink on the patio, but I canceled at the last minute to go instead to a meeting about the community farm. My friend was a demanding person and prone to ire, so when he didn't respond to my message, I assumed he was mad. And then I was mad at him for always being like this and let the silence stretch. But really he was just sick and then, no one would know for many days, but gone.

I knew him better than that. I am the one who expresses my anger with silence. He always came out swinging. Silence, after all, he knew so well, is what despots and their autocracies are made of.

Just beyond the faltering trees of this flood forest, an eagle circles the stretch of cattails that line the oxbow lake made by the river, which once wound this way, then pulled back. I watch how their faces spill open with downy pollen as the wind sways them. They are the between and they contain the between that passes up through their roots and down through their leaves.

I do not mean for this to be a metaphor. The cattails are themselves, passing through this world even as it passes through them.

Lecture Notes on Literature and Empathy

Empathy became interesting to me when the other professors in my English department began fighting over it. I hadn't given the word much thought before, just another word among words, maybe a bit woo-woo, but so ubiquitous I figured it was one more of the common feelings I don't seem to have, or at least don't have with very much intensity. But no, some of my colleagues said the whole idea of empathy was a racist construct. They quoted Solmaz Sharif. "Empathy means / laying yourself down / in someone else's chalklines // and snapping a photo." Others wondered how could this be, when empathy is the entire point of literature. Our mission statement says so. The room was tense.

Given that literature is mainly composed of made-up people, I joined the party describing empathy as another ego-protecting delusion of empire. Then I left the meeting so I could get back to my most pressing question, which for a long time has been: What is this feeling I get when I walk through a field of swaying grasses?

I thought maybe learning everything I could about how it feels to be a grasshopper would lead me to an answer. Which is how I found out they only become locusts when they are desperate and hungry. Drought settles in and they must range more widely in their foraging. They encroach on each other. And then they get touched too much. Each brush of wing or leg sends a shivering of hormones that begets more trembling and brushing and touching until they become red-eyed and swarming, fucking, screaming, brushing more and more in a growing cloud of each other they don't know how to stop.

Because I'm an English professor, I was trying to apply a phenomenological critical apparatus to my methods by approaching my experience of consciousness through the objects of direct experience. Whatever that means.

The white-man-ness of philosophy leaves a lot of gaps, many of them the size and shape of a uterus. So I googled "woman phenomenologist" and Edith Stein's was the only name that came up. She had written a book called *On the Problem of Empathy*, which seemed a long way from my question of grasses, but surely the synchronicity warranted a little humility, so I ordered the book anyway. And this book turned out to be the most useful explanation I have found yet of who we are to each other.

She proposes empathy is a pleasurable experience of research. This sensation of being "one with others," she writes, "does not give me the others, but presupposes their givenness." It is pleasingly reassuring, she says, to realize other people are as alive as you are, but that comfort is also an invitation to the difficult work of thinking and trying to understand them that must follow if you really believe your feelings and their beings to be real. Empathy, then, is the feeling that we're on the right track, not the feeling of having arrived at the truth of someone, which would be impossible, as such a truth, if it exists at all, is entirely their own. Even if they wanted to give it out, they can't, because of how our feelings are filtered into each other's, endlessly altered by the act of perceiving. Solmaz Sharif says she likes to replace the word "empathy" with "love" and see what happens—sometimes there is a greater truth, sometimes it makes the lie transparent.

Grasshoppers are happiest at the hot end of summer. The grasses are yellow and their stridulations fill the dry air. They fiddle lust songs and promise songs, food is here songs, all is well songs, and a host of other tunes biologists say help create social cohesion and encourage sustainable dispersal.

It's almost too much, how close the poets and philosophers and professors get. Some days I am filled with a foreboding shiver of how together we all are. Along the edges of the fields the grasshoppers sway, each alone on their bow of a bent blade of grass. When I pass by, they fly up for a brief moment, a little burst of yellow wings, their little clicking whir a song, a pulse, a buzz coming, it seems, from inside my own chest.

ONSLAUGHTS

In the forests of my childhood, invasive honeysuckle makes dense woody undergrowths that crowd out other plants of the forest floor. That is one way to explain the loss of chokecherry, serviceberry, inkberry, spicebush, and viburnum. Though another way to understand what is happening is that Missouri was logged three times over, then parceled out for monocropping by corporate agriculture, and honeysuckle is the kind of plant that is drawn to disturbed soil. It holds the banks and ravines and nitrogen and whatever is left of that once nutrient-rich layer of loam until the soil is not disturbed anymore.

A friend who does conservation work on Iowa prairies a few hours north told me about a huge fight she had with one of her neighbors out in the middle of the town's tiny piece of remnant prairie because of how he was spraying herbicides on invasive species. She was exasperated, enraged really, by the idea you'd pour poison in the ground to save anything.

She pointed to a grove of young black walnuts bushing up in the center of the field. That used to be one ancient walnut tree, but this neighbor got the Parks Department to cut it down because it is an invasive. With all of the extra sun, walnut seeds, which had lain dormant in its shade for generations, sprang up, even as the roots did what they do when the earth above them is laid bare, which is sucker forth new saplings everywhere the old tree had cast its shadow. My friend was dismayed at how much more prairie would be lost this way.

She cares so much, her neighbor cares so much, nobody

knows what to do. They just want to see the grasses grow. So they bickered and accused each other all the way back to the parking lot.

When we lived on a scrap of prairie in rural Missouri, I thought first occasionally and then often about leaving my husband. Though I grew up in the city, I'd never lived as far outside of nature as I did when we were homesteading. Our eight acres were an island in a sea of corn and soybeans.

Every weekend it seemed, Brian was lost in the woody strips edging our small field. First he went in with a hand ax, determined to remove every bough of honeysuckle. The next year he tried again, this time with a small blowtorch to burn the stumps and prevent them from suckering back to life.

Out among the black-eyed Susans and Queen Anne's lace I buried myself in the other side of the yellow honeysuckle blossoms he was hacking at. Basket in hand, I pushed deep into the brush, head covered in pollen, bees buzzing my knotted hair, to gather flowers I distilled to a syrup that was delicious to drizzle over biscuits. He could have spent his whole life chopping and never kept back more than a single glade, the circumference of the body of a deer with her fawns. He was just a man and the honeysuckle was an ocean.

It is not the nature of a prairie to stay in one place. They are slower than water, but have their own ebb and flow, following after the tides of grassfires and grazing buffalo. The forests follow them, more fires follow the forest, these succession cycles are as much what a prairie is as the grasses. All we have now are the last islands of an oceanic being.

After a few years, we gave up and moved back to the city, where we became better at loving each other and also our neighbors, which made us able to miss the land we'd left behind. One drought summer when the haze from huge wildfires to the north made it as clear as it had ever been that we were already at the end of the world, I became convinced fireflies had gone extinct. I drove Brian out to the country and refused to go home until I had seen one at least. Finally, where thickets of honeysuckle reached the water's edge, I saw a light and then three. Hardly more than that.

Though honeysuckle is not good for birds, there are more birds in woods with honeysuckle than where the honeysuckle has been removed, as their choices have been reduced to some kind of berry, or none.

The last day we lived on that farm I'd grown to hate for how small my life felt then, we took one last walk around the acreage. The path was lined with his blackened stumps. From the center of each a sprig of green wood sprang forth, bolting after the sun. He sighed at the futility of his work and I did too.

When I think of all the mistakes I've made in this life, though, I remember how we finally reached the glade he had carved with the blistered hands of what I thought was a futile obsession, a perfectionist's need to control. The ground in that spot was covered now in mayapple, a native species that grows across old forest floors. I hadn't come across one in several years. I reached beneath the broad leaf to see if there might be a green and tangy fruit for us to suck on as we walked. They were all gone—deer love a mayapple. They lower their heads down to the leaves and then reach out those muscular and agile tongues, long enough to curl around a single berry and pluck it from the branch, barely even rustling the tender leaf above.

Porcupine Grass, Green Needle, Pasqueflower, Mallow, Wild Rye, Prairie Dropseed, Buffalo Grass, Gama Grass, Wheatgrass, Goosefoot, Little Barley, Sumpweed, Erect Knotweed, Maygrass

I wanted to understand what it meant to return, to the land and to each other, so I went to visit a forager and prairie conservationist I admire for how she never settles for an easy answer.

The first time we met she taught me and my five-year-old how to make thread from native prairie plants. We busted open dogbane stalks she'd harvested at the end of their season and pulled out their long fibrous threads. We did the same with milkweed, but even more gingerly because their silk is so fragile.

This time we talk about the PhD thesis on a theory of conservation she suspects cannot be written, despite how she is writing it. The trouble is she doesn't mean conservation exactly, or sustainability, definitely not permaculture, which is just the word the 1970s back-to-the-landers chose so they wouldn't have to acknowledge Indigenous science. She says she doesn't want to be another white person describing nature either. I too have written in all of these ways and am wondering how to think otherwise.

Driving across Iowa, one of the headlines on the radio was that salmon in the Sacramento River, after such promising restoration efforts, probably went extinct during this latest heat wave. The dusk was rising and I was trying to remember when

I had last seen a firefly. At least two years, by my reckoning, but that couldn't be right. What if that was right?

When we used to live in the same neighborhood, she took the kids on foraging field trips. The way it often went: She led the kids into the fields and showed them a few plants, the kids quickly grew tired of cutting brown stalks and spent the rest of the morning throwing handfuls of burrs into each other's sweaters.

One of these children died while I was looking after him and now I never stop looking for him. Sometimes, for a moment, it feels like I've found him. When a sparrow's wings set the tall yellow stand of Jerusalem artichokes swaying. Or when my child stomps up the stairs with elaborate thuds and arms dragging, a kind of theater they don't remember learning to mimic from him when he wanted the adults to know how annoying they are.

The visit with the forager was a pit stop on my way to revisit one of the few herds of buffalo on one of the last remaining scraps of prairie left in Iowa. Buffalo and prairie grasses belong to each other. When the grasses are grazed down they undergo a physiological change called compensatory growth and come back thicker, faster, fueled by the nutrients in buffalo slobber left dripping into the soil around their roots.

This conservationist had recently started raising goats with an idea they might be able to eat back invasive species and fill some part of the ecological niche buffalo once occupied on this land. I pulled into her driveway late, night already on us, but she'd only gotten back herself a few minutes before.

Three goat kids still mewled from pet carriers in the back of her truck. She handed me one that was sopping with pee from her long drive and I felt it soak in my shirt as I cradled the poor baby. Older goats came to bang at my thighs as they flocked to sniff at each new arrival. They were ridiculous with all of their nibbling at my flannel and nuzzling at the backs of my knees and I loved them. It had rained all afternoon but now the stars were out, heat lightning lit up the field like a strobe, and the grasses pulsed wildly with more fireflies than I had ever seen in my life.

I thought buffalo went extinct because all of my childhood history lessons said they did. But only almost. They can still be found, here and there, across the continent. There are sixty, give or take, at the Neal Smith Wildlife Refuge off Iowa-117 and when one breaks off from the herd to come close enough to stare back, it feels like being held in the eye of a god. I have been trying to remember whether the kids were bored or reckless or terrified when we drew close, but the only part that comes back is how that great beast held my gasp in the depths of his black pupil.

On the Green Line

Like a lot of people, I don't always know how to ask for help, so I offer it to someone else instead.

Though I hardly even drive anymore in this new city, I keep glue traps in my car because I hoped I might again see the woman who was so upset about spiders in her bedroom. She seemed to be hallucinating, but I once had a spider infestation in my home and I woke up every morning welted, itchy, and freaking out. Wouldn't it be nice to see someone I shared an hour with and be able to say *Look, I heard you and I found a way to help.*

Mycorrhizae spores form vast underground networks, to sip at the simple sugars photosynthesized down through the roots, and in so doing connect trees, who then share their resources within and across species. Douglas firs and paper birches shuttle carbon back and forth seasonally, with birch giving most generously in the summer when their canopy covers the forest and firs returning the favor in winter when they have all the light and more.

Yesterday on the green line, a young woman was having the most distressing high I have ever seen. She was so fast, her head and her hands, her voice a kind of song in a sharp key. It hurt to look very long at her arms.

I was coming from a meeting about what will happen to a person I have cared about. The agenda included a pamphlet for me about orders of protection and forms to erase my home address from all public records. I have not decided what I will do next, but yesterday I decided to be one of the people who carefully and consciously never makes eye contact with a person in a precarious position.

Not forever. I hope this is not who I am forever.

The artist Jenny Holzer once rented a huge marquee. She stood on a ladder and slid black letters into illuminated rows: *It is in your self-interest to find a way to be very tender*. Sometimes when the train blurs past, I think for a moment that is what these billboards could be saying.

Mushrooms are such beautiful and elegant reproductive structures of a much larger subterranean being called fungi. When they emerge as ripe bodies after a rain, it is a consequence of how full the forest is with vitality and a green light filtering through the leaves into the fungal loam. Wouldn't it be nice if we could see some right now? If there were a crack in this concrete and some haymower or puffball or shaggy ink cap pushed through the tender dome of its head just to see how things are out here in the air?

In the Distance a Phainopepla Flies over the River

I don't want to talk about the affidavit. I want to talk about the relationship between beavers and the willows who spring back with two branches for every one a beaver chews down. How the willows hold the river winding through the desert that holds them all. But I can't seem to explain without talking first about the three hundred JPEGs of screenshots, or why the Office of Public Safety wouldn't put a security guard near my classroom. How one of the reasons is that I am a woman who had the gall to first ask for and then demand it. Another, someone said, off the record after a meeting, was that they couldn't afford to provide security guards for all the women faculty on campus who ask for them. A reason I wished were on their minds, but knew wasn't, is the danger increased law enforcement presence on campus poses to minoritized students. In time I would learn that the way to handle a committee of white men, when you are a woman, is to ask your solution in the form of one helpless question after another, and then wait with quiet patience until they think of your solution for themselves.

I want to describe the way the grasses grow in the shallows and how it is their swaying in the current that gives the Verde River its greeny glow. But I'm distracted instead by how it is to wake every day to another Facebook post where a young man who once called me mom, like a joke at first that turned into a plea and then a promise I could never keep, describes a new violent fantasy about watching me die or watching me watch him kill every student in my classroom or watching me watch him commit suicide in front of a room full of students so everyone will know what a bitch I am. Or saying he's sorry and he loves me. Then posting once again that link to the video where one man shoots a bullet through another man's hand.

For so long I couldn't say anything at all. Though I tried. To get away from thinking about my own fear, I focused on everyone else. I went to protests and public hearings. I came to the school board meeting about changing the name of Robert E. Lee Elementary with a pocket of notecards I planned to use when my turn came. But I never spoke, because the way these hearings work is first you state your name and address into the microphone for the record. I didn't think it would help this cause or any other to state my name and then the Safe at Home ID number on the little blue card provided by a government office for keeping my address out of public databases, and, if I was diligent and devoted hours to phone calls and forms, off websites like whitepages.com.

My former student, who had aged out of foster care just a few months before he started college, lived in his car parked in a campus lot during at least one of the semesters I taught him. For a time he was a person of interest for the arson that destroyed the bathroom across the hall from my office. Most likely, I'd been told by a representative on the threat assessment team, he was a disorganized schizophrenic. The disorganized part was reassuring because his fantasies were complicated. He probably couldn't get the gun or the bus ticket or hack the registrar's website to find the time and room number for my classes. But you don't have to be very organized to type "Kathryn Nuernberger address" into Google. You do have to be extremely organized, however, to keep the answer from turning up.

I knew I would not and could not speak when I went to a hearing about State Representative Cheri Reisch's letter of admonition to our neighborhood public library for being in violation of the state's new gun laws, which permitted her and anyone else to keep a gun in a pocket or purse or holstered to their chest as they walked anywhere at all, including to public forums in the library meeting room where she had responded to constituents' concerns with a firearm in the bag at her side. That law prohibited so much as a sign asserting "No guns allowed here." In a tiny conference room at the same library, I came to bear silent witness on behalf of my friends, who had prepared remarks. But we were such a small group that a librarian passed the mic one by one down the row. So I felt I had to say my name, and then said, "I cannot tell you my address because in another library in this state a young man is sitting on a computer posting links to snuff films on YouTube and then describing the ways he is thinking of killing me. I am here today because I'd like for us to find some way to all be safe." And though I wish I hadn't, I started to cry, because it wasn't until I heard the words spoken out loud into the public record, until I had seen every face in the room turn stricken, that I understood how bad things had become.

I want you to know that I watched members of that library board wipe tears away from their own eyes half an hour later when they cast their votes in favor of removing the signs in the building. I want you to know I understood they were right that if they had voted any other way the state legislature would have withdrawn their funding and the state courts would have closed their doors. I want you to know that people with mental illness are far more likely to be victims of crimes than perpetrators. I want you to know this student tried to find a place to live and a doctor to help him. That we searched together on the computer in my office. That the residence hall director said, maybe truthfully or maybe not, that they had no space left. That he told me how he had, like every semester before, received $9,000 of financial aid in the form of a single check and he'd already given most of it away to people he wanted to be his friends. He spent the rest during a manic episode on dozens of books he thought would help him understand what was happening to him.

I want you to know my student exhausted the ten free counseling sessions provided by the student health plan. And that the assistant to the vice provost told me he would make some phone calls to see what he could do to find other options for counseling and housing. I want you to know that at our next conversation, after the fire in the bathroom, the assistant to the vice provost would say he was sorry, but he forgot to make those calls.

I want you to know that it is reasonable and common for a person to spend one night in a shelter and be afraid to ever go back. I want you know it seemed for a moment like a lucky break that my father's nonprofit work included a client in that very town who was building a sixteen-unit apartment complex for low-income people with chronic mental illness. We consulted with representatives from that nonprofit about what could be done to help my student. But they were sorry too, nothing could be done at that time. I want you to know that six months past too late, I went to the ribbon-cutting ceremony for those apartments and I was proud of my dad and glad, despite everything else, to be in the company of new residents and health care workers celebrating together. I want you to know I understood enough about how things get done inside a broken system that I clapped politely when Republican Congressional Representative Vicky Hartzler gave her speech and cut the ribbon, I did not spit in her eye or say a word about how she voted against Medicaid expansion and every other social services funding bill that might have hired a person or created an office that could have saved my student at any point between the moments when his father went to jail, his mother lost custody, his first foster parent hit him, and the day he died at age twenty-five.

I want you to know that when a student emails you in the night to say they are having suicidal thoughts, the university website has a number you call. After that call comes a cascade of events outside your view and your control—a wellness check, involuntary commitment to the hospital for a three-day hold in a psych ward, medications are given, sometimes he is then released, sometimes additional services are available, sometimes eight or ten or sixteen weeks in a residential treatment facility with steady medication and therapy, leading to improvements you presume based on how the death threats stop for so long you start to think they've stopped forever, but always the funding runs out, the prescription ends. I learned through my many conversations with social workers and counselors trying to help me or him or me and him, how each new torque on that roller coaster makes this kind of disease meaner and harder to treat.

Somewhere in between one system failing him and another, I changed my phone number, the university expelled him, the car he'd been living in got towed, winter came and he got arrested for breaking into strangers' cars for a warm place to sleep. Somewhere in this time I moved five hundred miles away to a place where it would be even more confusing for a disorganized person to find me. A place where it would also be harder to find myself, a stranger now among strangers. And then my former student died, of overdose maybe or suicide, it is unclear, but he did not take anyone else with him. I want you to know it is true I was relieved and I also want you to know it was not the ending I ever wanted.

Only with several years of hindsight could I see that I began researching mutualisms because I wanted to lose myself inside relationships that engender more abundance, more beauty, more life. Sometimes I described my project as finding systems that actually work. This was why I drove for two days straight to reach the Verde River in Arizona to be among the willows, which grow mingling among cottonwoods along the riverbanks and floodplains. The willows have evolved to sucker, so they flourish when beavers chew them down. The more trees the beavers fell, the more branches spring forth from the stump left behind, and in this way the beavers and the willows love each other. The river too evolved, to be held in its banks by these trees, to pool and pond around the beavers' dams, which store and conserve water, creating habitat out of desert for many other creatures.

But while I nodded approvingly at each trunk I passed, gnawed to a point and framed by sprigs of new growth leaping from the wound, it was a bright yellow sprig of stiff leaves that obsessed me. No matter what angle or lighting I tried, my plant ID app only had obviously incorrect suggestions. Occasionally an error message said: "This may be dead." None of my googled descriptions or thumbing through field guides helped either.

What I held had fallen, it seemed, from a very tall cottonwood. More of these unidentifiable ocher leaves, thick and branching and stiff like coral, were all over the grass beneath the green canopy. I craned my head to look up into the tree and peered along the banks of the river. Where had they come from?

The morning I took our dear old dog to walk along the river, I puzzled over these branches while she waded up to her knees and drank huge lapping gulps. Back at camp I leashed her to the picnic table so she could enjoy the nice breeze and the view of the water below. I did not realize as she lay down on the gravel that she would not get up again. There were bluebirds dashing in the trees and a skunk shuffled on the far bank.

Hers was a peaceful death in a beautiful place. When I miss her gentle, so quiet and so slow company, I am grateful for that.

When I miss her, I remember how we decided we would need a dog to bark in the night so I could sleep again, and Brian came home with the biggest, most intimidating animal at the shelter, a 130-pound Great Pyrenees. He had not noticed how frightened she was at first, had not expected how she'd hide her massive bulk behind my knees when anyone, even him, even children, approached. When she let us come close, we could see the little nubs of her front teeth had been filed down so she could be used as a bait dog, a body on whom more ferocious animals would be forced to become more ruthless than their instincts allowed. And then we understood the claw and teeth marks scarring her back beneath the softest fur we ever felt.

I had not thought it would be comforting to care for a dog as afraid of every sudden sound and passing car as I was, but it was a comfort to be together. There are some creatures who experience something terrible and are made by it more gentle and kind than they otherwise would have been, though it was not this way for me. I blamed myself for having been so naïve when I sent emails saying things so easily misinterpreted as "I care about you." For the hubris of thinking I could save someone. I stopped asking acquaintances how they are really, stopped making eye contact with vulnerable people in public places, stopped checking on students who seemed off in class that day.

Some days later, walking along the river, it came to me. The strange branch must be a mistletoe. Desert mistletoe is a snot-colored vine, common in the southwest, found clumping up in the cottonwood trees where the phainopepla, a silky flycatcher with gleaming black velvet feathers, eats its berries. Only after it has died does the plant become this gorgeous mustard yellow, the kind of color kids paint an orb of sunlight.

The blurring whirl of yellow leaves I spin between my fingers.

I have been too slow to see the good in people.

I have been trying to change.

I have been trying to learn how.

For so long, if I spoke at all, I only spoke of that time with outrage. I had anger and anger to spare—for the overworked and overwhelmed assistant to the vice provost, for the campus cop who handed me a brochure about self-defense classes I could pay to take, for the elected officials voting their party lines, for the neighbors who voted them in, for the neighbors who did nothing to see them voted out, for the man I worked with who said this was why he didn't let students tell him their feelings, for the other man who said maybe I was overreacting, for the colleague who said men get stalked too, for everyone who didn't know what to say. But once, hours after the latest pointless meeting where university officials again denied my requests—security for me, housing for him—I emerged at nine p.m. from my night class into the echoing hallway of the emptying building, squaring my shoulders, keys held as a weapon in my fist. And there was my department chair, sitting on a bench at the far end of the hall, grading papers. As if this were normal. As if he were not watching for anything at all.

My chair, like me, was just an English teacher surrounded by people who needed more than he had the power to give. The campus and the town were small enough that I knew he would have missed his eldest daughter's volleyball game to be on that bench. That his wife was the kind of person to leave a plate for him on a counter to put in a microwave. He and I never spoke of his presence, just nodded and said good night as we left the building together.

When Fiona died, my dear friend sent me a note. I asked her if she remembered the first day I walked Fiona to pickup at the little backyard school she'd created for kids like ours, kids with genders and religions and IEPs and broken hearts our red-state school officials couldn't seem to understand. I worried to see one of the children approaching. This kid's gait was unsteady and she did not always respond to adults quickly the first time they spoke. Like so many of the students there, I'd seen week over week how she'd transformed from someone silent and afraid into herself. As she approached, Fiona tucked in behind me, and I worried a cornered dog might bite. But before I could reach out to stop her, this child had laid herself across Fiona's back, across all the scars, and pressed her face behind those soft ears. Fiona stood perfectly still, then leaned into the embrace. At the sight of this, all of the kids came running, calling her polar bear, petting whatever corner of her body they could reach. Even the child combing through her shaggy tail, a move dogs usually find too aggressive, she accepted as the awestruck homage it was meant to be.

If you study any particular mutualism for very long, you soon find yourself studying the entire ecosystem around them. Each individual choice contributes to patterns, which in turn make future individual choices possible or not. I traveled so far to the Verde River so I could imagine something besides the extinction cascades in the place I call home, the ones caused by the concrete of human dams piling up feet of silt and oozing mud over rocky creek bed shallows where pallid sturgeon once laid their eggs among the crawdads and mussels, mayflies and frogs, all depleted now, or entirely vanished. My student's pain came at the center of such a barren waste, one he sometimes was making, sometimes trying to unmake, even as it was making and unmaking him. That this can never be changed is unbearable.

What also is: Where the dams have been removed, the beavers beget the willow groves that beget the riverbanks. There is mistletoe in the grass, falling from wide arms of the cottonwood branches overhead, then a moment when that rare bird, celebrated for the gleam of his ebony feathers and striking silver crest, lifts with a sudden leap and gasp, the outstretched wings of his silhouette into the air, a belly full of seeds he will cast over the desert as he passes, a glimmering desert just beginning to pond and pool.

What Is Past

George Washington Carver was fascinated by the yucca, and why shouldn't he have been? It sends up narrow, sharp-tipped leaves like a ring of swords around stalks as tall as a person, which drip with heavy bells of flowers in early summer. As a teen, he won a prize for his fine watercolor of a yucca in bloom. As a young scientist, much of his early research focused on this plant.

Yucca has long been scientists' favorite example of obligate pollinator mutualism. Though there are more instances than I could ever list, this is the one illustrating passages in textbooks about plants that can only be pollinated by one creature—the yucca moth, whose mouth and tentacles are all perfectly evolved to fit with a click into the pollen-soaked stamens of a plant that will, in another season, feed their larvae a portion of its seeds. To study this relationship is to come to know an entirely different way of understanding gardening, farming, and belonging to the plants that feed us. Carver devoted his life to finding such ways of being with the land.

These three kids I love, one who is mine and two who feel like they almost are, were running through the woods of the George Washington Carver National Monument outside Carthage, Missouri, where Carver had once been a child among these trees. According to the informative plaques that begin in the visitor center and then stretch out dotting the paths, Carver was a moody little boy, always disappearing into the copse beyond the fields to draw plants and write poems.

According to these plaques, his mother died in uncertain

circumstances, on the run most likely, but kidnapped, the signs say, at the height of the Civil War. She died in a skirmish with the men the Carvers sent on horseback to "rescue her," the signs say. And then the Carvers took the baby who came back alive to raise as their own. Like parents, the signs say. But the Carvers were enslavers who owned his mother, the signs don't say, so they took him as their own like enslavers. I don't know how to fully imagine the hurting fragile confusion of such a childhood inside everything these signs don't say, but even the glimmer I can see is a terrible ache.

According to the plaque outside the gated cemetery where the white Carvers are buried but George is not, he always spoke well of the people who raised him. Anyone can see what a sinkhole of history the storytellers at this place have created. And yet, the fact he should be named here at all is a rare degree of memory to encounter in rural Missouri. The day before, twenty minutes north of here, we dragged the kids to the Joplin History & Mineral Museum. They thought the miniature circus was cool enough until I remarked on the racist caricature of the Man from Borneo and just generally got going about exploitation as the driving force behind the very concept of sideshows. Then they sighed and wandered off to look at the display case full of cookie cutters. It's so fucked up that my husband is writing a travel guide to a state where the NAACP has issued a travel advisory. It's so fucked up that I'm here for it.

I asked the woman working the ticket counter about Langston Hughes, who was born in this town. I couldn't find anything on my first pass through the exhibit hall, but it was a teeming collection, so a photograph or a pair of eyeglasses or a first edition of a book of poems would be easy to miss. The woman at the counter said they didn't put anything of his up because the town "wasn't so nice" to his family so it didn't seem right to claim him. That's how the people here describe the 1903 lynching of Thomas Gilyard and the subsequent flight of nearly every Black family that lived in Joplin then. "Not so nice."

The path out of the Carver National Monument visitor's center winds into the cool shade of the woods where a statue of Professor Carver as a child gazes into the trees. He grew up and found over three hundred uses for peanuts, which was the research that made him most famous. During the war, when supply chains made rubber almost impossible to obtain, he worked with Henry Ford on a project to make tires out of goldenrod. When he was a professor at Tuskegee University, he got on Booker T. Washington's nerves by constantly asking for more money for himself, his lab, his department, insisting his research was more significant than that of his colleagues. The letters read like every pleading email I've ever sent a dean, every grant I ever got funded. He embraced the absurd audacity his profession required. In addition to the work with peanuts, he also found over one hundred uses for sweet potatoes.

Now that he's dead, he is as much the child who painted a beautiful yucca as he is the distinguished professor whose botany was a balm to hungry sharecroppers scraping at the nutrient-depleted dirt cotton had starved into dust. Now he is his whole life.

One of these children I'm watching is the same age George is in this statue. As the wind rustles through this grove, I'm thinking of how much he must have missed his mother. And whether that hurt too will last forever. I'm thinking of how he was the scientist who realized peanuts are the kind of plant that can replenish barren land because they have a symbiotic relationship with a bacteria that live in their roots and return nitrogen to the soil. Then I hear one of the kids calling. "Come see! We found something poetic!"

When I reach them, they are standing on a rough-hewn bridge across a trickle of creek. The water runs clear as sky over the pebbled bottom. Willows bend down to let the fingers of their leaves trace the water as the sun scatters her little glints across the ripples. It feels like the kind of place where a ghost might sit down and take off his shoes, then rest on the bank for a while, watching that light.

To reach the yucca, you must keep walking, beyond this woods, across the fields to the ridge where the soil is more rocky and dry, where the sun is so bright you have to shade your eyes to see the moths fluttering to find each other, their pollen, a perfect place among the open blooms, exactly the way George had once painted them.

ALLEYS

Weeding cuticle deep in the loose soil mounded around the zinnias at the community farm and my hands tingle with the breathing of all these transplanted bacteria, protists, fungi, and archaea grafted to the packed clay of land that carried a convent on its back and a gravel pit in its belly for sixty years.

I might not feel it so much, this ecstasy of a microbiome, if I weren't trying not to miss the place I came from, where I loved the elder and wild carrot, yarrow and goosefoot, but did not know how to live anymore either with the flags my neighbors loved to fly over their soybean acres. I was trying to pour that missing into hope I might someday come to belong in this neighborhood where the volunteer coordinator is growing Thai holy basil for her Hmong family and neighbors, while one of the farm managers checks the Jerusalem artichokes every day because she heard its tuber tastes like a potato but can help lower blood sugar. She got tested for diabetes herself the other day and is telling us the way that white nurse stabbed at her skin like she thought Black people couldn't feel pain. But mostly she's just worried about her father, who might lose a toe to diabetes, or worse.

In general I keep quiet, as gentrifying newcomers should, but once in a while I'll offer something I think might be a gift. As we pull wild lettuce, which got out of hand and now towers above our heads, spewing its downy fluff into our faces, I tell how this plant was once used to treat hysteria. It has sedative and slightly hallucinogenic properties. We laugh at this like people who might be hallucinating a little. The farm manager then pulls some wild mustard—*Look,* she says, holding up the thin bundle of small yellow blossoms lost beneath the lettuce. *This is one of the great mothers.* Her ancestors, and maybe mine too, cultivated it to become broccoli, brussels sprouts, cauliflower, and the whole rest of the cruciferous vegetable family.

It was such a moonlit beam of blue lights flashing across my kitchen window that night, before we knew what had happened. It looked like we were all living together at the bottom of the ocean.

I was up late, reading abstracts in JSTOR about mutualisms drifting beneath starry waters off the coast of Hawaii, wondering how much of her microbiome the bobtail squid feels when the bioluminescent garden of *Vibrio fischeri* lit up in that organ behind her eye. Is it suffering or elation to spume 95 percent of it into the open water, where the bacteria will mostly die but some drift into the bodies of younger and more empty squid who sense they need something but don't yet know what it will feel like to be answered with a city of light?

When morning came, the dog and I walked our usual circle through the neighborhood, picking up a bouquet of zinnias from the farm along the way. As I passed through our alley, over the debris of yellow police tape, my neighbor was taking out the trash with a gun holstered to his chest. This kind of brandishing has never been his way before, he who opens his garage with its flat-screen and homemade bar on game days and also fills the block with the smell of deep-fried tacos for three dollars every Friday. After he told me what happened, I handed him the bouquet and he tucked it in his shirt pocket, frail and pretty beside his revolver.

He must have been so afraid. He must have had no idea what to do. The back doors of our houses look at each other all day long, but I didn't hear a single one of the four shots, each aimed at his brother-in-law, but grazing without apology anyone in the way. He is pissed at his brother, calls him an idiot for what he is mixed up in, but thank God that fool is still alive and everyone else is too.

The squid use the light to blend in with the moon shining on the water, or they shut an eyelid and disappear completely into the depths. They can reflect and refract and direct their light in all directions. But, like any living being, they have to learn how to do this and they may not always know precisely the most perfect way to cast that glow. All they can do is try, and hope there will be a chance to try again.

On Error

Beyond the stained glass glow of the library's windowed wall was a garden of medicinal plants. Purple bells of foxglove and yellow buttons of calendula flourished among the leafy blankets of chamomile and sage. For a summer I worked at the mahogany table where the man who invented the pacemaker once took tea.

My fellowship was for researching quack medicine, particularly as it related to matters of electricity and the heart, but on the first day I was scolded for using the word "quack." One curator said it was a judgmental pejorative that misunderstood how important unproved theories are to the development of knowledge. Other fellows objected on similar grounds to "pseudoscience," "dead ends," "mistakes," and "folk." It became hard for me to say, when asked, what exactly I came to that place to learn.

Fortunately, there are many distractions in the archives. I followed a little question about luminescent aether into the whole history of hot-air balloons. Then nosed around in a box that contained the indecipherably calligraphic notebooks of a man who had been institutionalized for fifty years. His grandniece brought them here after he died because she didn't know how, but was sure they mattered.

I read with more or less derision the self-published account a farmer-scientist wrote about his experiments with a greenhouse constructed entirely of blue glass. Though his findings were not significantly for or against the light, he chose to print them on blue paper. Every time I turned another heavy, ink-saturated page I thought of how carefully he would have lifted each delicate pane into the frame of greenhouse like he was holding a piece of the sky.

I live about one hundred miles from that farmer's land. The winters up here are very long and dark, but when the gray months came, this man walked among his seedlings beneath a dome of blue.

Independent of these largely unread results, whole schools of thought in both psychiatry and the visual arts have emerged around the idea that our moods and capacities are influenced by the light we receive.

I hate learning. For my whole life I will never stop being wrong about what I used to think. It is such a painful and humiliating way to live and only the alternative is worse.

Where do storks go in winter? One dumb beautiful theory was that they turned into mice. Another, that they went to sleep at the bottom of the sea.

After

Before lichen, there was no such thing as soil, no such thing as mud, nothing we could call a riverbank. Water just slipped across the rock fields of the earth. There was no such thing as death then either.

How to explain to a child? How to explain to myself? When Death came into this world, he was born from the sporocarp who lifted up and puffed a whole body's worth of spores into a drift of wind. How strange it must have been for him to once have been all of the loam and all of the roots and the sunlight trickling down through the ichor of the trees and now to be only himself, separated from the rest by a name like Black Knot or Elderberry Rust or Old Man of the Woods.

I always have the hardest thoughts in the morning. Some things I will never be able to explain or understand or accept or live with, so I try instead to imagine how it feels to be a lichen, to be an alga so laced through with filaments of fungi you are become an entirely new kind of being.

Lichens live beyond fables and science and the very idea of understanding. They spread across the name on the stone, making a soft green, breathing and being of whatever light and dew pass across them, whatever of the fading earth reaches through.

After a disaster all is barren and smoking and the air is dust for a while. Then, across the sharp and ragged rocks, lichens.

The History of Disrepair

Augury: The ancient art of telling the future by watching the flight of birds.

I tell him, "It's such a shame true love isn't real."

The wrens make a racket with their singing, but I hardly notice it most of the time, walking around as I do, so expansive and tar-shingled, red-bricked and clay-piped with all those little wires and switch plates and hardly even knowing my own attic-nested rafters.

He says, "It is to me." And I fall asleep with my head on his chest.

Wrens like us for our rubbish and always have. They're old friends, or would be, if we were paying attention.

We used to find abandoned cabins on every hike we took. The roof would be gone, the furniture too, all the glass, but still we would find at least one and up to three of the following: a black Sunday suit, a handbag, a teacup, a blue jar full of buttons, a toolbox, a closet still wallpapered in pretty roses.

There comes a time, after many years, I tell him, "It's a shame true love isn't real," and he agrees, "It is."

When Genevieve Jones, the nineteenth-century ornithologist, painted a nest—and she only painted nests, sometimes eggs, never the artfully posed corpse of a dead bird—she made a list of all the materials the nest was made of—ribbons, copper wire, horsehairs. But when she painted wren nests they were always just sticks, feathers, and a little straw, which is boring, so instead, she listed all of the places she'd heard of wren nests being found.

And I say, "What?"

A buggy top, a beehive, an old boot, a hat, the pocket of a coat.

He says, "I'm afraid I'm becoming those things you hate—predictable, repetitive, intransigent."

The wren never repeats the same song twice when he courts. Later he whispers his songs to his mate when she nests.

I say, "Stop it," and he says to let him finish. "It is to me."

I fall asleep with my head on his chest like a heart beating in a shoe, the morning light pouring into a cup of porcelain and straw and feathers.

Some theories of augury:

There is a god and the god speaks through birds.

There are birds, they are one kind of god.

There are birds. We used to speak the same language.

Against an Apocalyptic Vision

In those falling in love years we hiked often to one cabin or another, all crumbling into ruin. We'd eat our lunch with legs dangling out an empty window frame. I always liked when we could open a closet and see the bright bird-and-flower wallpaper that had once decorated all of these gray and yellowing walls.

I try not to be afraid to say what is real. I try not to hide behind the convenient narrative. You could say we fell in love, but it would be more precise to say I followed him through one door in the woods to another.

There was one place, reduced to a square of foundation and a chimney, surrounded by hundreds of daffodils, their faces following the sun as it passed from the cabin over the path and down again to the creek. The wind blew through them and it was hard not to think that for a moment I saw the glimmer of a woman in a polka-dot dress kneeling in the grass with a trowel in her hand, a basket of bulbs by her side.

When I'm afraid all I have is hurt, that I ruin everything if I stay too long, I think about her.

A few years back the cabins were all burned down by the local forest service rangers, and I have grieved them, as I do the pallid sturgeon, the hellbender, the nimble wills, the wake-robins, the ebonyshell and sheepnose mussels, all gone from this place.

If I were to bet, I'd say they were guys with badges who liked the feeling of setting a fire. Or the world is terrifying so they cling to a narrow definition of order. Or maybe they just don't imagine much at all. They said the cabins were being used to cook meth, so maybe they saw something awful and burning down abandoned houses on overgrown homesteads in a forgotten county of a failing state made it seem like they'd done what they could to help.

Susan Stewart wrote a philosophical treatise on ruins and one of her theories was that a ruin's emotional impact occurs in direct proportion to the permanence of its materials. This theory does not account for how it delighted me to come upon a splintered one-room cabin, maple tree growing through the last slats of roof with a vulture taloned to the shingled hip like a heartbeat ready to leap.

When he proposed to me at the top of a ruined fortress carved with impressive permanence from the side of a mountain, I found the wreckage uninspiring—just stones and dust and sun. But later that day we wandered in the woods at the base of the mountain. These were young trees reclaiming the geometry of what had been a wheat field. A glint of metal caught his eye and he reached into the leaf litter to lift out a scythe. It was flaking chunks of rust, but its heft and moon shape were nice and also it seemed to remember the grass in a way we might come to remember each other.

Stewart does say some things about ruins that ring true: "In a ruin, a formerly closed view will be opened to weather, light, earth, and sky, and our awareness of what was once present will be more acute because of its absence."

Somewhere the sky is orange on fire. Here, between the pile

of stones where a great-grandfather was born and the trickle of a wet weather creek, it is only a thin gray. So I lean my head on his shoulder, feeling what we've lost and also what of us remains. I wouldn't have it otherwise, of course. Because we couldn't. Because it's futile to hold anything against time. Because of the swallows and pipistrelles, barn owls and house martins who prefer our buckled eaves and crumbling chimneys to nest. Who flourish in our wreckage.

THE SPACE BETWEEN US

Perhaps it will not make sense to you, but to me the answer to loneliness has been to reread Antoni van Leeuwenhoek's letters on protozoa to the Royal Society of London. The answer to the way every perfect moment collapses in on itself has been to study his descriptions of what he observed using the microscope, a clumsy new technology that he, a humble glassmaker, perfected and then grew obsessed with using. In the first letter he describes the stingers of bees. Later: lake water with its green spirogyra algae, the plaque between his teeth, skin cells, sperm cells, protists, rotifers, blood cells drifting through the capillaries of an eel.

Between the hours I spend among his pages, I have been watching video footage taken with a very impressive lens. *Argulus bengalensis* has burrowed its hooked mouthparts into the gill of a fish's cheek. It has grown fat on mucus and sloughed fish scales and now lets go to drift in search of a mate.

Even though *A. bengalensis*'s eggs can gestate in the nest of a single drop of water, it is useful to remember those eggs are as thick with yolk as any. The mating pair had mouthparts connected to a set of antennae that together formed a hooked, spiny proboscis they used to sucker into a fish's operculum and feed. To find each other they had to detach from this host and swim with their four pairs of thoracic appendages awkwardly attached to the carapaced oval of their bodies, peering around the water with pronounced compound eyes. Watching them this closely, I can almost imagine how their life feels.

Sometimes I don't know how to keep being here. Many people

have told me I should focus on parasites instead of symbionts, because that is what humans are. How far away these people all seem, how close I feel instead to this lonely glass grinder writing letters to kings and princes and czars about what he found putting his scabs under glass.

So small, *Philodina roseola* experiences water as a gelatinous substance she must crawl through with her cilia, which are not quite arms or legs or anything a human knows how to feel. She has come to eat of these eggs laid by *A. bengalensis*. The camera cuts and we too drift over this nest of eggs. They are as small as a drop, and yet each one is fat with yolk and albumen, like any egg you might crack or scramble, carry within yourself or lift, poor broken blue shell, from its dent in the grass.

Once this was a parasitic relationship that made *P.* fat and *A.* scarce and then vice versa. Like how there are rabbit years and then fox years then starving fox years then rabbit years once more. But they changed. As all relationships change over time. In general, the parasitic ones become symbiotic or they go extinct trying.

Now *P.* exercises restraint, only eating open the eggs to free a new *A.* and another *A.* and *A.* and *A.* and *A.* and *A.*, which spring forth into the water, hungry already for a fish to sink the hooks of their antennae into. The eggs can't hatch without the help of *P.*'s feeding teeth.

Because there is no way to live without each other, as they hang from that fish's face, they too will become hosts to nematodes burrowing through them into the jaw and then down into the fish's intestines.

The fish is a home or the fish is a god or the fish is some barely conceivable dimension or wasting away on the hook with guts full of worms or the water is glowing tonight with bioluminescent algae or the glittering spume on the waves is the souls of mermaids extincted you could say or maybe they've just never been understood by human eyes to be what they are.

Against Morals of the Story, Against Delusions of Purpose, Against the Dry Husk of a Self-Aggrandizing Charity, Against Prudery and Islands and My Own Hard Shell, Against Lonely Fear, Against Easy Narratives and Rigid Taxonomies, on Tenderness

The ant is close now. The rove beetle curls up his hind end and abdomen as if his whole body were a tail. The ant lowers her head to smell, to taste gingerly with forelegs and antennae. She is trying to understand the beetle's appeasement gland complex, an entomologist would say, though I think it is more precise to describe what is happening here as pleasure and yearning.

The beetle reaches back with his antennae to tap, caress, taste the ant's face and the conversation progresses. The ant finds more glands along the sides of the beetle's body and licks their secretions. Then, overcome, she grabs the beetle by the hairs that run alongside these glands, which have grown for precisely this purpose, and pulls the beetle back to the nest in a frenzy. The beetle is willing.

In the nest the ants feed each other tenderly. A hungry ant caresses another's face and they align their mouthparts with a clicking hiss before one regurgitates whatever food she is carrying into the other. The beetle's mouth is also a perfect fit. They have all evolved together to give and receive such a kiss.

Once accepted, the beetle lives among them, fed this way, perhaps a parasite or perhaps the secretions are essential to the community in some way. Perhaps the beetle is narcotic or the ant is beatific. Perhaps the pleasure of being together is the advantage and the reason and the point.

Mermaids

Ants horrify because their hyperorganized societies are so visible to the human scale while any individuality they may have is largely illegible. Which makes it very upsetting to consider how much we might be like them. From that fear of economic systems, authoritarian regimes, and our place in the endless drone of an industrialized society, it is difficult to make room in the story for their erotic and tender longings, their secret lives in the mouth of a flower. It becomes easy to forget we are all living in outer space and have been this whole time.

A great many orchids, the endangered lady slipper for one, expend a portion of their energy creating pseudobulbs. This pouch at the throat of their stem quivers with the coming and going of an ant colony. They invite these guests because ants spit a kind of formic acid that helps keep their soil the perfect pH.

This is an example of myrmecophilia, a way of being in a love relationship with ants. Though I think it sounds like how I love mermaids, because of the myrme- of their tails glimmering in the moonlight and then the -philia of the kinds of unions I wish were possible and maybe even, if I keep trying, will discover they are.

The myrmecophiliac caterpillar invites ants to slurp its syrups—ants who raised him from a grub massage, tickle, lap at his dorsal nectary. It is a dangerous pleasure for all. The caterpillar must transmit chemical appeasement signals through the milky nectar to keep the ants from suckling the skin right off his body. He beats and thrums warnings by drumming himself against the earth when the ants become too exuberant in their thirst.

I don't know how to enter the mind of an orchid or a butterfly, a farmer or a commodities market, but I know mermaids are a kind of beautiful catfish monster. Like an orchid, her songs radiate across galaxies in a pitch human ears would find unbearable if they lived long enough to hear the song echo back. An ant could live lifetimes inside that note, as could the *Glaucopsyche lygdamus*, the silvery blue, touching her antennae to the air above each leaf as she tastes for a site in ideal relation to the colony to leave this egg, which will become in time a grub the ants will find to take in as one of their own.

STRANGERS

Pitcher plants grow one tall and elegant leaf that curls itself into a tunnel with a lip that stands just barely agape. It is a long hallway of a plant with a door that does not quite close—voices murmuring forth whisper an entire lifetime of half-heard and misunderstood secrets.

A carnivorous plant, the pitcher lures flies into that gorgeous throat with a scent of rotting nectar. Then a bat comes and slips its delicate tongue, perfectly evolved to lick down into the ichorous belly to feast on the half-digested soup of insect prey. It leaves behind nutrient-rich guano in exchange and together the pitcher and the bat are nourished and satisfied.

Where I live now, too far north for those long-tongued bats, pitcher plants fill whole bogs with the gardens of themselves. They are smaller than their tropical cousins and their symbiosis is only with a single species of fly, who lives as a larva floating on the tiny pond of digestive juices until it is ready to helicopter out of this familiar womb into that strange sliver of blue at the edge of the known world. Once fully grown, the fly will return to pollinate and then lay eggs in the plant that was once its home.

Brian, who I love in part for how easily he knows what people mean and what they want to hear, says I should talk less about microscopic creatures. He says anyone can relate to bats, but no one cares about the larvae of a fly. I care, I say. Of course *you* do, he sighs.

I didn't throw myself into years of researching mutualisms and relationships because I understand others well. I did it because I don't.

Many times I have watched bats flickering at the edge of a streetlight for the slow length of a falling dusk. It is not easier to imagine their world constructed out of clicks and echoes than it is the fly's view through a thousand optic nerves and receptors, each pinprick stitched to the others in a sensation of one continuous whole world.

When the first pitcher plant of the season has lifted her face from the thick mud of the newly forming earth, I pull Brian down to see. As our knees grow damp on the moss, I lift up the lid of leaf to show him how the dew and rain mix with the plant's own enzymes. He seems charmed, perhaps by the plant, more likely by my urgent and messianic lessons about such inconsequential things. But he's trying to feel the bog as I do. And I'm trying to explain it in a way so he can meet me here.

Here. In the tiny pool at the heart of a leaf, whirling with dying and feeding, becomings you can hardly perceive and barely understand.

A Definition of Longing

I was alone on a lip of island, looking across the blue of sea and gold of sand to the shadow of a mountain rising above its mist. There monks invented an iridescent yellowish-green liqueur and named it Chartreuse for the mountain that gave them each of the elixir's 130 leaves and roots and blossoms. I held the little bottle of it I'd bought from the gift shop up to my eye like a telescope and watched the sky turn the color of yearning.

I love to be alone. But how I missed the shimmer of something green. And the feeling of being known.

On another outcropping of monastery, brothers concocted verdigris ink by submerging copper in wine. They wanted to achieve the leafiest possible light. As I gazed into the emerald ink reflecting back beneath flickering fluorescents, I missed you terribly. And wondered who this you I lean after like a vining plant even is.

I've gone anywhere and everywhere to try to find the other shore of my missing. The redwood glades have a gilded green light that feels like falling in love. I have lost myself to it more than once.

In the lab, banana slugs eat any sapling the researchers offer, except the redwood. They eat cardboard, but not redwood. They are revolted by redwood maybe, or in awe of it. I doubt the trees think very much about the slugs who let them grow so tall, though it is becoming clear to me who the gods of this evergreen sky really are.

A redwood tree will live for a thousand years; a banana slug will last seven, at most.

Covered in an extraordinary mucus, they ooze on the single foot of their bodies, which glisten a perfect chartreuse on the thick mossy log. After they mate in their hermaphroditic fashion, they eat each other's penises in order to detach.

I am reminded of Aristophanes's description of perfect human love in Plato's *Symposium*: Soulmates live eternally connected, cartwheeling their synchronized way through life. He said it like a joke about how impossible our ideals are.

All the other drunk philosophers laughed too, then concluded with great seriousness and sincerity that love is an orb, a kind of planet, floating through some other dimension but casting its shadow on us.

When I watch the slugs I become as slow in my gaze as they are. How tender it must be to let go of each other by feeding each other. How much the touch of my own eyes are the selfsame squish and slime of slugs on a bough.

You belong to some other planet. I am here alone. These beautiful disgusting snot beasts are somewhere between.

A Kindness of Sparrows

How strange it must feel to be yourself, a bird, and also carry within that self a soul of the dead. Of course, that's just fairy tale gossip about sparrows. Of course we're all doing that all the time.

I've been watching the sparrows closely since they are the only alive thing I can see from my window. I listen as they plan their days of slipping between worlds. I have studied them from within my silence for so long I think I know their stories.

One is laughing at how they aren't people at all.

Another at how invisible they can be.

That one is telling every single secret she ever heard.

This one is making up a little poem that projects all her feelings onto zoomorphic human figures—you can tell her it's not scientific, but she doesn't care.

I made a promise to myself that I would not use metaphors when I write about other beings. Because a metaphor erases half of its equation. Because a metaphor presupposes a universal relationship to language that only serves the power elite. Because anthropomorphizing keeps you from seeing beyond yourself.

But there are good reasons to think otherwise. Metaphors are the language of the spirit and dreams. A metaphor can be the stitch that holds our disparate worlds together. A good metaphor increases the connections across creation.

While I'm not sure I need human terms to understand sparrows, I'm certain I need sparrows to understand myself.

After the accident I did not talk to anyone for a long time. I blamed myself and expected everyone else would too. I don't know how or what Erin knew to have sent me that postcard: "You are loved, you are loved, you are loved," it said over and over, like a flock. Her lovely feathered handwriting filled every inch. I slipped it in my purse that day and since I have nowhere else to put such a gift, it stays in that pocket, growing more wrinkled. Often I forget it is there and then find it, this kindness, all over again.

A sparrow knows that words don't really matter, but also they can, a little.

One of the old metaphors of sparrows is that they are harbingers. That, like any of us, they carry in themselves a great abyss. That, like any of us, each is the embodiment of an abyss that decided to try being for a while.

When a sparrow catches your eye—for a moment they fall utterly silent, like someone who knows what it means to be caught in the eye of sorrow. Then the whole flock turns to pity, the gentle chirps and trills and wing-rustling, trying to call you back from whatever long moment you were trapped inside.

Loneliness

Purple rosettes bloomed from the mosses and piles of reindeer scat made from moss and turning back into moss at the same time. An oxidized blue-green bullet casing lay among the sprigs of yellow grass pushing through the swelling and dilating cracks of permafrost.

After bleeding for days I dreamed I was still pregnant. The heartbeats were so loud in my ears. I dreamed that all I had to do to save a child was open my eyes. Sometimes I stood on the deck of the ship, looking at the glaciers that made this fjord, ancient and now almost gone, and wondered if there is a reason I am here. I'd try to remember something I said in the fellowship application about the communities of krill and fish that gather beneath the protective bell of the lion's mane jellyfish, a creature expanding its range as waters warm. But all I could think now was no, there is no reason at all.

The kind stranger I shared a cabin with asked me as I started to fall asleep if I was terribly sad. I said if I let myself be sad over things I think I could have changed, there would be no bottom.

On shore that day we had filled so many bags with plastic trash we had to send one of the Zodiacs back to the ship with no people, only waste. From the raft that trailed after, I watched the little plumes of diesel chuff from the engine. The photographer from Finland said it would all eventually be incinerated in Sweden. A couple other Americans were talking about how good it felt to give something back. I felt another blood clot slip from my body into the heavy pad. I was afraid of what I'd see when I went back to my room.

I'd wanted to be alive, not like the moss flourishing beneath each vertebra I lifted at the ruins of an old poacher's camp, but like the walrus I saw raise his head from the deep, the ones I'd sometimes hear singing through the hull beneath the water where I could forget there is no such thing as night here, that there won't be for a long time. Ocean acidification makes sound even more transmissible, their bellows come from further away than ever, across the chaos of ship engines and the massive quakes of falling ice into these dreams where I tried to hold armfuls of mist inside my body.

On deck, after dragging myself from stupor, I realized every other passenger and the entire crew left the ship to its anchor and went back to shore for a bonfire made of the many driftwood logs that fell from Russian cargo ships decades ago. Beyond them are the ruins of the research station where scientists gathered data that proved the earth is not a perfect globe, but more like a slightly deflated ball, a little flatter at the poles, which is why the warming waters here will eventually stall ocean currents and jet streams.

How strange I must be, I realized. Even on a ship of artists and scientists, all eccentrics in their ways, still I am the only one who chose to stay behind, tied to the unknowable depths. I watched their shadows dancing around the fire. Some of them were entangled, kissing, I guessed, or slinging arms over each other's shoulders as they passed a bottle of vodka. I could hear the guitars carrying on the wind. I did not feel lonely, as I would have imagined I would, as so many of them would have believed I must be. I felt happy to be so close.

Beyond their party, in the gap between the mountains, a thin strip of pink glows steady at the horizon. Somewhere hundreds of miles to the south, someone is waking up to a rising dawn.

Everything Is Going to Be Alright

Every day I wake up and read about, think about, write about, creatures who need each other, who know how to need each other. I also read about parasites, who haven't figured out yet what they can offer in return. A symbiotic mutualism takes eons of coevolutionary adaptations to reach sustainable balance. Even then, they often require a third-party parasite to keep the relationship from spilling beyond what it can hold.

I used to feel harshly toward parasites, but now, knowing how they are in the process of becoming, I only have tenderness.

Oak trees are constantly parasitized, the cicadas are down there suckling their roots, their bark endlessly penetrated and eaten through, galled branches, bellies full of acorns everywhere all around them. And all they get in return is this teeming forest made of and being themselves.

At a rest stop on the edge of the Brood X cicada emergence, I overhear my kid in the loft of the RV saying to the Zoom screen, "I don't have anything to else to say, I just like looking at your face." And then, "I like looking at yours too."

Each individual cicada is a swarm unto themselves. They have endosymbiont bacteria, one is the *Sulcia* and one is *Hodgkinia*, living in their guts turning tree sap into amino acids the cicadas need and cannot produce any other way. A cicada, living so many years underground, unmoving, just suckling from the roots and waiting, must be so familiar to themselves. The *Hodgkinia* have a tendency to evolve rapidly—they divide into genetically distinct beings, sometimes in just a generation, and each distinct being makes only one of those essential amino acids after that. One researcher summed up the situation as "fragmenting in a ludicrous way."

The first article I read made it seem like another apocalypse. The cicadas have to barf on their eggs to ensure they receive all the *Sulcia* and all the *Hodgkinia* they need. But with the *Hodgkinia* so subdivided, a cicada could barf and barf and never be sure the young were getting all the necessary combinations.

I don't want to live in a world without cicadas.

I used to think it was important to tell my child only the truth. After the hives every night and the doctor saying it was a common response to stress and trauma, I told the story we all need to believe if we are going to live. "Everything is going to be alright," I'd say as I tucked my kid in. My sweet kid who saw their best friend go under. Saw me fail to save him. Who couldn't go to school because two thousand then three thousand people a day were dying in our country of a virus. My poor kid who didn't know, but maybe did, about the prescription their father started after he told me he sometimes went into the basement and thought about firing the nail gun into his head. Because he couldn't stop thinking there must be a way to make the world fair. I'm so afraid my child won't be able to love this life. I'm afraid of this for all of us.

In the last brood emergence in Asia, a species of Japanese cicada was found carrying *Ophiocordyceps*, a fungus best known as the zombie virus for the way it parasitizes insects and forces them to do things like climb the tallest grass blade so a bird will easily see and eat them, allowing the fungus to reproduce in the bird, which will soon die of them, bringing these offspring back to the earth where there are more ants to infect anew. In the cicadas, though, *Ophiocordyceps* has replaced the *Hodgkinia* and live peacefully in their digestive tracts for generations, turning the xylem from tree sap into amino acids for the cicadas.

When they emerge from the soil, cicadas are called nymphs. After they shed their skin they are called imagoes, which is also the word for the unconscious image of one dearly loved. I watched an imago breathing its new body open once. The edge of the wing had a band of green that was so bright and neon I couldn't compare it to any other color I'd ever seen in this world.

On the Other Side of Ending, There Is

I have been reluctant to say what I know of the American chestnut. Because one of the rhetorical functions of an expression of hope is to promote complacency and the maintenance of the status quo, a kind of lie. But hope is also the feeling that holds us here when nothing else could.

The entire canopy of forest over my head was flaming pink. Where I expected green leaves there were blushing flowers and labial flowers and flowers drooping their dewy petals like a grandmother's perfume. I took out my phone and started googling to understand these fantastical circumstances at the top of the mountain. When I looked down from the ridge I could see lightning flickering through the clouds below.

Mountain laurel trees bloom briefly but extravagantly for just a few spring weeks. The rest of the year they grow their hard wood into impenetrably dense thickets. Their undergrowth is an equally impenetrable sea of ostrich ferns, which crowd out all the other plants. Locals call places like this the laurel hels. They are only beautiful if you don't know they were once interrupted by chestnut trees, who grew huge and could withstand the fires that once swept through these forests every twenty years or so, clearing out the undergrowth and making way for greater biodiversity. Or they are only beautiful if you can love inside a confused tangle of grief. Or they are beautiful until you remember there is a child who should be alive and maybe that means I should not be. Or maybe a child should be alive and everyone else should be too, the laurels blooming alongside us as we gather nuts from beneath the fronds of fern below.

I try not to lose myself inside thoughts of what should be. The American chestnut went extinct from a blight caused by invasive species and overharvesting a century ago. Only not quite, because their stumps keep suckering forth saplings. Every once in a while such a twig lives long enough to set seeds before the blight takes it too. I hope it is not wrong of me to say the chestnut may yet come back.

Down a trail that traces the sandstone bluffs I used to walk every day, but now have driven as far from as I can get, a trickling stream runs through a ravine beneath an eagle's aerie into the lake. I have in one hand a carving of a wolf and in the other a heart the kids made by chipping at hunks of the soft stone you can find in that place. Somewhere on that bluff is another carving. It wasn't his name and none of us quite remembers what it would have been, but it is there, a word or a shape, tucked among all the other graffities, some fresh or mossy or fading as the rain works them away.

I have heard it said that time is not a line but a sky, stretching beyond and then laying the fog of itself down through the trees and then through us. Moments are not before or after, but drifting past and all around each other. He's not here, but just over there, look how he crouches on a rocky ledge to reach the place where he uses one stone to shape another.

‘Ūhini Nēnē Pele

I have been going to sites of aftermath to see who can live and how among the ruins. I do this, I tell the people who provide the grants, so I can learn something useful about how to live and love and survive and save from within the sites of our own destructions. I do not mention how much I myself feel like an aftermath.

I went to the slopes of Kilauea looking for lava crickets only found on the barren fields of a recent lava flow. They are extraordinary beings, appearing it seems from nowhere after the end of the world to live on proteins in the spume of the waves that rise up from the sea. They make no sound, which is why my friend the animal behaviorist keeps going back to study them. She wants to understand how they find each other.

The Hawaiian people have of course known these creatures for as long as they have known the lava and call them ‘ūhini nēnē pele.

In the stories my people tell, crickets are the old ones who stay up all night recounting the whole history of the world. The chirping of crickets, our mystics say, is the first sound you hear after you leave your body.

Brian, who used to collect water samples and count macro-invertebrates for our coalmine-ravaged watershed, came with me to help look. He's the kind of person who will lift every rock in a field before he gives up, while I quickly grow distracted by the spackling of lichens that return with the crickets when the ground is cooling. I wander to the ‘ōhi‘a lehua tree at the edge of the field, which is the next to come back, their pink inflorescences blooming so bright against the black earth, their roots burrowing through the thin dust between the stones to make them soil once more. Beneath my feet the hardened ground still seems to swirl. I follow a scorched white tree from its toppled crown to the deep hole where the lava pooled a long time among its roots. In the depths, small but very green ferns grow.

The heat of the sun was becoming too much, so I convinced Brian to try the method my friend had used the first time she stumbled on lava crickets, by accident while researching another insect. Like her, we grabbed an empty wine bottle from the trunk and baited it with cheese from our cooler of snacks and left it sideways among the rocks. These days she prefers to use plastic bottles and bread, though she doesn't want me to give more details than that, as she worries about tourists harassing the crickets.

Then we left to walk a spiraling path through another field where native Hawaiians had carved concentric circles into the rock and buried their newborns' umbilical cords. The generations of markings looked like a map of the stars. Acknowledgments of guilt are so useless, and yet I feel I should say it was my government that stole this land and my people who became and become and keep becoming a people who only seem to know how to look for the ends of the earth.

On the other side of the mountain a new lava lake boiled and oozed. Night fell. Brian and I had sex in the rental car like teenagers. I wished so much then that there was a way I could be at the beginning of something again.

The bottle was empty, as we expected it would be, and I was glad not to have caught a cricket. Even though we would have put it back on the ground after holding it a moment, I realized I had not really come here to see them, who I'd already seen in Tupperware in my friend's lab. I'd come to see everything else that made them and everything else they had made. Above us, the moon was as full as I'd ever seen, the air smelled of smoke and a coming rain.

Back home, my friend taught me how to find katydids in the field near our offices. I don't belong here either, but I think if I keep trying to learn and unlearn and give more than take, maybe someday I could. Before we began walking our path around the perimeter of a small pond she pointed to the low grasses and clover and said that humming is the crickets. She pointed to the higher branches of trees—there you'll hear the cicadas. Then she gestured to the middle distance. Among the milkweeds and goldenrod, the katydids would be singing. I found it almost impossible to distinguish any of these songs, but every now and again she would hold a finger to her lips and follow some pitch to a blade of grass. Often the first katydid she found was a silent female who had also been creeping on the song. Then we'd sit very still waiting until the male forgot us and resumed his chirping. Farther off, my friend could make out a catbird mimicking, sometimes the traffic, sometimes the hum of insects.

Although I nodded along, trying to be in the same moment, the truth was that I could only hear the crescendos and diminuendos of a single huge song, while my friend drew one strange creature after another from the field and set them on my hand so I could admire each for a moment before they leapt once more into the chaos of chirping and wind-rustled grasses.

The Nest, the Seed, the Egg, the Spiral

Between two people there is a wasp bothering the edges of a stretch of blue sky. There is a green hill and, beyond, a mountain fading into the horizon. Snow is falling far away at the top of the mountain between two people. A plane flies across the space between them. Rain begins to fall. Droplets catch on the unfurled tongues of an orchid and then slide down the purple-spotted throat. The two people glance at each other for a moment, then away.

The fig wasp queen pushes into the fig through a hole so small she rubs away her wings and antennae as she goes. It is like the reverse of being born. She is covered with pollen from another fig and as she writhes through this one, laying her eggs, she rubs pollen into the plant's ovaries.

The fig is an urn protecting hundreds of tiny flowers, an inflorescence, all turned inward. When I look inward I find a confusing and pulpy mess. When I look outward I see faces I can't understand. The two people glance at each other and then away.

It is too hard, they think. They may be right. What do I know, after all, of what lies between us, except that when you look in someone else's eye, you see your own face looking back, though even closer and in yours once again is theirs, an infinite holding that is passed back and forth and back again.

The fig wasp queen lays eggs on many, but not all, of the flowers within the urn. Flowers brushed with pollen become seeds, flowers holding her eggs harden into galls that provide food and shelter for her growing larvae. The queen dies and is digested by the fig.

In time the males hatch. They mate with their sisters by pushing their seminal vessels, which are almost but not exactly penises, through the walls of the galls. After, they eat an opening wide enough for the females to escape. Then the males keep eating, opening a pathway out of the fig. They widen the hole that once tore their mother apart to reach the air, then fall, wingless, to the ground and die.

The females crawl over the flowers who have opened with them. They gather pollen before reaching the pinprick of light at the top of the universe. Then they open their wings and fly into it. Out there is the whole world, full of meaning. A world like a fig turned inside out. A world like a fig turning in on itself. A world trembling with memories they can't quite remember and now they are burrowing back to the beginning, where a mother is held in the fig, yes, and where the fig is not even a seed but the idea of a seed, held in the cradle she makes of her thorax and abdomen and all those legs wrapped for just a moment around a flower's anther.

How the Mussel, How the Fish, How the River, How the Mountain

The foot of a mussel encounters a crevice on the cragged bottom of the world. It oozes itself to create a vacuum, then radiates a sticky foam that congeals, even beneath the water, into tethers about the thickness of a human hair, which hold the creature fast. These golden byssus threads encircle the mussel like the haloed rays around a pietà. The mussels cover the stones first, then each other, becoming a new bottom on which the algae and crawdads and eggs and larvae will make themselves.

I am told it is tedious when I talk about mussels, because what is the point? So I will interject to say that I am, like you are, living in a time of endings, which makes it comforting, as well as practical, to consider how things begin.

The river is only the river after it has flowed through the filter of their bottom-feeding bodies—mouths which are their guts which are the foot and sensory system and reproductive organs, all one muscle wrapped around the dark ventricle of a heart. The fish is only the fish, the shad only the shad, after their eggs have drifted into the shelter of an Altamaha mussel's slightly gapped shell.

The mussels become more mussels by sending up sacs of larvae camouflaged as worms. A fish comes to investigate and the throb of bundle explodes in a frantic cloud of burrowing for the gills, the throat, the eyes, to feed. The fish itches and staggers. Weeks pass and the mussels grow large.

It was hard for me to talk to the biologist about these creatures because she kept describing their life under the deepening water and not so long ago I took three children I love to swim in a pretty bend in a quiet river and one of them drowned there.

In time the mussels, fully grown, will let go. In time the fish will swim on. And so it will go, again and again, like a beginning.

There was a story I used to tell the kids about a stonecutter who wished. He wished to be the crew boss and the wish was granted. Then a king. Granted. Then the sun, then the clouds covering the sun. Then the mountain pushing through those clouds. All granted. And then, at last, the wish to be a stonecutter bringing it down once more.

I used to think it was wishing that would break your heart. Now I just think about how the sunlight was so beautiful on the water, it doesn't make sense. That river winds around and around the place where I live. I can't go anywhere where the creek is not running over the stones, the rain is not washing through the leaves down the sides of the street. I am a ghost now, for my mistake, am nothing more than wishes upon wishes, but sometimes I forget and feel the meat and soil of my life for a minute. I am sorry, and you have all been so kind, saying accidents, saying anybody could have —

I would like to go back to the beginning, when I was a little girl sifting freshwater shells no bigger than my fingernail from the gravel on a bank so much like this one, wondering what had once lived in the pearlescent blue of such cupped palms. Somewhere beyond, I can't quite remember, but I know not far, my mother watches me. Or maybe she watches the water, or the sun filter through the leaves overhead, how dappled all the light.

THE BARRENS

$$\left(\frac{P}{B}\right)_i B_i = \sum_{j=1}^{n} \left(\frac{Q}{B}\right)_j B_j DC_{ij} + E_i + Y_i + BA_i + \left(\frac{P}{B}\right)_i B_i (1 - EE_i)$$

Waiting atop bluffs at the edge of the sea, I scroll my little screen like an idiot, in search of a pleasurable connected feeling, even as the whole ocean crashes below me. I come upon a scanned snapshot from the '80s where a young woman has slung her arm across the shoulder of a teenage boy holding up huge purple starfish, one in each hand. Behind them the sun is setting into the water.

What's so interesting, my friends want to know. They have finally come to join us at the end of this trail through pine trees, ferns, blackberry bracken, banana slugs, and skunk cabbage. It's nothing, I say, pushing the phone back in my pocket, and we begin the climb down to the shore. I have come here to think and write about the concepts of keystone species and extinction cascades. Though largely abandoned by ecologists now in favor of more precise terms, Robert Paine proposed these field-changing terms after watching how the decline of starfish in a region led to a monoculture of blue mussels in the tide pools. Paine marveled at how the loss of a single species could so radically transform an ecosystem. He devised an equation for whether or not the world can go on after such terrible losses.

When my friend's son finds a starfish, all of its legs still supple, its suckers flexing with each rush of incoming tide, we hold the kids' hands so they will not be tempted to touch. We tell them this creature is very special, but do not break their hearts with why.

I have seen the data in the preliminary reports suggesting the pandemic may be abating, or the starfish may be evolving a new resistance. I'm afraid to hope. I am afraid to break my heart with even so much as a wish this might not be the last starfish I ever see.

I have a memory from my own childhood that I open in my mind so often I must be careful now not to tear the creases. Tiny starfish wash up all along the beach. Some still have soft arms and these I rush to throw back as far into the waves as I can. But most have passed into pretty little rocks I add to the pile in my bucket.

It has been so many years since I've seen a healthy starfish, I sometimes wonder if I dreamed that day, my parents under an umbrella at my back, my little brother up ahead bending to lift his own treasures from the water.

Sometimes when I'm making the short drive from the preserve nearest my house, one so thick with prairie flowers and grasses I still learn some new plant's name every time I walk there, I cross the bridge into the outermost ring of suburbs and think, ah yes, now we are entering the human barrens.

I've been passing through barren after barren, driving from one ocean to another, making my notes and observations, trying to understand what a relationship is.

Barren, which means emptiness and waste, also holds abundance, too-muchness, the way a species can overwhelm a place. The gardens of the Pacific tide pools have, in most places, been turned to blue mussel barrens. Pine barrens overwhelm the biodiversity of a mixed hardwood forest. Laurel hels are a barren that sprang up when the American chestnuts died out from blight. The blueberry barrens of down east Maine are a vast coastal region where sandy acidic soil and heavy fogs make a habitat where blueberries alone seem to thrive.

Barrens, because European colonizers couldn't figure out how to make farms of these acres. Barrens because they saw no use for the carnivorous pitcher plants and sundews that populate the marshy lowlands between all those berries. Barrens, because uncultivated land, by colonizer logic, is barren and belongs to no one, and thus not only can, but should, be clear-cut and transformed into useable acreage for monocropping or a new condo association. Never mind these are far more barren than a stream running through a deep green and muddy bracken.

It was densovirus, warming waters, and ocean acidification that decimated the sea star populations. In deeper water the urchins, who had once been prey for those missing stars, reduced the kelp forests to barrens.

Not an equation, but equally helpful to my emerging understanding of relationships and friendship and grief is the Aboriginal concept of Bir'yun, which, according to Deborah Bird Rose, theorizes that "shimmer, the ancestral power of life, arises in relationship and encounter, so extinction cascades drag shimmer from the world."

I am not sure whether the urchin barrens are really barren or not. They are the end of the kelp forest and we don't know what they are the beginning of. There seems to be a resurgence of once-threatened sea otter populations now. They float on their backs pounding urchin shells open on their bellies, then feast. They were once creatures of the kelp forests too, sleeping entwined in the leafy branches so the currents would not carry them away. Now they have more urchins than they could eat in a lifetime and only each other to hold on to when the waves come. They don't know what the future holds either.

There is a caption beneath that distant acquaintance's photo I gazed at like it was my own tender memory: *My brother died twenty years ago today in an accident. I never stop missing him, never stop loving him.*

Let grief be grief, let urchins be urchins. We turn from the tide pools to the wide expanse of sandy beach. The sun is shimmering across the water we step into, up to our knees and then our chests, floating on the waves that carry us, time and again, back to shore.

Little White-Winged Moths Fluttering Everywhere

The white wings of the yucca moth drape a long way past their bodies, like a bishop's robes or a cathedral or some ghostly nun. I almost turn away, having lost all interest in beauty that makes you think about faith as a public performance of power. But then I zoom in on the mouth, where the single proboscis you'll find on most Tineidae has been replaced by three tentacles unfurling like a hallucination.

The yucca plant and yucca moth are considered by ecologists to be the iconic example of obligate pollinator mutualism. On summer nights the flowers open and the moths mate inside them. Then they use those strange mouths, which perfectly mirror the three anthers of the flower, to gather pollen, tuck it under their chins, fly to another blossom to pollinate its stigma, and finally lay an egg there. I question how much difference there is between that which we call ritual and that we call instinct. Once hatched, that caterpillar will eat through two of the seeds the yucca has made, but always leave a third behind. It is such a careful balance, one that took both species millennia to learn.

During these cool, dormant months, the caterpillars are grubs in the dirt among the roots of the yucca. You can only see the moths in the form of their echoes—the way the burst yucca seed husks trace the absence of those tentacled mouths. I drove eight hundred miles in the dead of winter to Texas with no more of a plan than to sit in the desert and think about this mutualism. I wished I had come earlier or waited longer so the moths themselves would be here. I wished I was not such a selfish fool, driving an RV that gets eight miles to the gallon in the middle of a pandemic in order to learn something about how creatures live together.

I wished, and then I realized I could not see Alice. I kept telling myself the kid was fine, just around these rocks or that bend, but I also knew I could never really know that.

But they were fine and then we walked together, stopping often for a scramble into one juniper tree and another. It had been almost a year since Alice had been anything like a child. But on this afternoon, reaching through the branches as before, I was relieved to see that beyond the fear and grief of losing their best friend, still somewhere in there was a kid. As I took a picture of that face peeking out from the juniper, Alice said, "He would love these trees." We were quiet together then, feeling how he might be swinging his legs from a branch just beyond the next curve of the trail.

The moment was interrupted by a woman calling. First "Hello?" Then, "Help?" Her voice had a note of playfulness in it. Did help mean help? When I didn't answer right away, she tried again, very serious. "Help! We're lost!" So I called back. She was funny, kept hollering "Marco! Polo!" until we met in the trees, but the situation was surprisingly dire. She was an eighty-year-old woman and her husband older than that. Though wearing sturdy boots with a trekking pole in each hand, they'd been lost for hours and had no water.

I offered to go find someone, but they preferred to follow us down our path. It hadn't seemed like a particularly hard route up and they were fit for their ages. But retracing our steps, every turn of an ankle in a narrow pass, every lip of root we used as a stair, made them falter. I saw, watching them hold each other, how frail a body can become.

None of us had bothered with masks. We, because we had expected to be alone. They, because no one here did that anyway, the woman told me, brushing aside my apology.

At first I was afraid to take her elbow, that I might give her the virus. But once, watching her teeter on a steep spot, I thought fuck it and reached out to wrap my arm around her waist.

I wanted her to know she could lean on my arm again, so I told her how we'd seen almost no one for a year to protect my husband, who has a lung condition. But that only seemed to give her the thought that she could infect me and she would not let me touch her again. I thought how I should have known she'd react that way and said something different. And then I reminded myself, as I sometimes must, that no one wants my guilt or my regrets. So I walked on, as if we were all fine, just near enough to reach for her or her husband if there was need. I sent Alice, who was still happy to be leaping among the rocks, ahead to scout all possible paths among the scrub and then come back to lead us along the easiest one.

The woman kept calling me an angel. I knew she could trip or collapse at any moment. Increasingly I considered how she might die out here. It felt like I might be leading her into that death. She repeated it again, "You are an angel."

It can be so hard to understand the moment you are in. Beyond the canyon's rim I watched the distant ribbon of a river that had carved this place. In those months, some part of my mind was always standing in a river, asking how could I have and how could I have and how could I, always looking for the danger I hadn't seen coming.

At last we could make out the parking lot below, but what a steep climb down. The woman was tearful with fear and exhaustion. The man did not speak, only stared. We watched as Alice hop-skipped from one boulder to the next all the way down. "Like a mountain goat," the woman said wistfully.

I offered again to leave the couple here while I went for help, but they had their eyes on the falling dusk. So instead, I stretched a wide bent-legged stance across two boulders, my arms out, ready to break a fall if I could. And I watched their legs tremble. His trekking pole buckled beneath his weight and he threw the bent rod down. It tumbled past me and lay across a bush below. This is another emergency, I thought as I squatted deeper to give myself more stability, and here I am again, making all the wrong decisions.

But they reached the bottom safely. Of everything that could have happened, this is what did. They hugged each other in relief, then the woman turned to ask me if I pray. Before revising herself, remembering, I think, how people like me—liberal and northern and city—are. She said, "I mean, can I pray for you?" I saw how she was trying to understand me and also give me what of herself she had. I don't think we can offer each other more or better than that.

I've never accepted a prayer from anyone in my life, but anymore who am I to say what or which of our helpless fumblings might matter? "We take all the blessings we can get," I answered. I was still surprised though, when she began to pray out loud, right then and there, that we be followed on our journey by ten thousand angels to protect and keep us. She prayed they gather round us, hold us in their sights, follow us wherever we go. She said she could see how we were surrounded even now by their light. She looked at me and said, "They are all around you now."

As we were driving away, Alice asked, "That was really weird, right?"

"Yeah, it really was."

"Do you think we saved their lives?" Alice asked.

How I wished that could be true.

"No," I said. "They probably would have been fine either way."

And since my child did not ask more, I did not have to say what it was that made me feel so held, still, as I drove on.

UMWELTEN

Winter Crane Fly

If I were a winter crane fly, my blood would have antifreezing chemical properties. Should light flicker across the eyes at the top of my head, suggesting the air is sunny and just above freezing, something would come alive in me. If I were female, I would slip among the swarms of males to mate. After a long time living as a grub, this frenzy would be one of the defining moments of my life. I would not live long as this flying version of myself. This sun on the snow, the crisp of the air, none of it would fit inside everything I grew old as a larva knowing of rotting logs and dead leaves, root burrows and mouthfuls of soil. I would not be human, so I would not philosophize the experience. So many cells and ganglia would be humming my new flying body. Somewhere in this cold woods a maple tree has been wounded and sap runs down its side. I would like to lick it, but like angels have no genitals, in their final instar winter crane flies have no mouths. And yet I am drawn, data proves it, to these places where the world is sweet.

Katydid

Night sparks along the threads of my antennae, tingling into the nerve bundles behind my eyes where, like a human, I keep my sense of knowing. I keep fear in my belly, which is bright red. If you startle me, I will fling wide my wings in a spasm to reveal this belly, the sight of which is designed to make you feel as if you are the one bleeding. I like this clever power about myself. I love the leaves on an orange tree better than is good for me or you or fruit or land. I love to hear a male rub his smooth wing over his richly carved wing. He is born carrying this shield etched with every battle he ever dreamed. I hear him throbbing across the grass in my foreleg where the tympanic organ, that hide drum of my own taut hind leg, beats his song back through me. In the same way I hear the water rippling on the pond and the wind shushing through the bluestem. Petalfall has begun and soon I won't fit inside this shell of a body.

Pine Processionary Caterpillar

If I were a pine processionary caterpillar, I would not like it. Though I would not have these notions of "I" or "liking." I would just follow the silk coming out of the caterpillar in front of me as the caterpillar behind me followed the silk coming out of me. Or maybe I would like the way it feels to be myself and also a train of three hundred or more, a cursive being in search of some other tree whose roots will feel like home but also different, because we are feeling like ourselves but also different.

If I were a pine processionary caterpillar, I would wrap that silken trail around and around myself as I burrowed into the soil. I would melt in there entirely down to goo. I would have to lose everything I ever was in order to become a creature with wings and a frantic urge to fly and fuck and lay spike-covered eggs among the pines as fast as possible. Sensing perhaps that this is the only day of my winged life and it is slipping away.

The Limits of Human Feeling

Umwelt is a concept developed by the biologist Jakob von Uexküll, who was trying to explain perception and why it is that perceiving feels like reaching from a place of deep loneliness to touch someone. Umwelt holds all the meaningful aspects of the world for a particular creature. The mind and the world are inseparable inside the circle of umwelt because the mind interprets the world.

When two umwelten interact, this creates a semiosphere. In a semiosphere the world does not exist objectively to be sensed and experienced, but is a structure where thinking and the things you think about operate together to produce sense and experience.

Sometimes I will look at a critter very closely for a long time, wondering how it feels to be them. This experience of noticing an umwelt other than one's own is called umgebung.

It is a common sensation among humans to feel as if it is possible to know someone else, anyone else, as you know yourself. It is one of the great pleasures of our beings to feel as if that sphere around me is growing to include you, and anyone you ever understood. We've been known to take it to the point of delusion. It's hard to stop, it feels so good, this *Who are you?* emerging in our minds beyond the place of questions and problems, breakups and funerals. It's hard to contain the magic of realizing that there is a you, you are not me, and here we are, beside each other.

The Twitch

The green-striped mapleworm becomes the rosy maple moth, which is sometimes pink-and-yellow-striped, like a candy or a pair of mittens on a child. Their lives are divided into something called an instar, of which they have five. In one, their heads are black. In the next they are yellow. Later they will be red. Between one instar and the next they grow horns and spikes along the sides of their back. In their last instar they burrow into the chambers between the roots of the maple tree.

When I touched the cocoon, I expected something silken. But a cocoon is just another form an exoskeleton can take. The moth is not in there, she is there. And when I caress her ballet slipper of a body, the cocoon rustles away from my finger, while I too pull back, startled to have met this being, alert, awake, alive to everything beyond herself.

Epithalamiums Are a Bullshit Poetic Form of Wedding Toast All Full of Lies About What Life and Love Are Supposed to Be, Here, I'll Tell You the Truth Instead, a Gift, I Hope

I want to begin by telling you of these tiny frogs called microhylids who live beneath the legs and in the nests of huge tarantulas. Not because they relate to this occasion except that I was thinking about them all the time in this year when you were getting married.

Like a frog I am here like you or any of us because of how I wefted and warped a kind of evolution inside this all-together nest I like even as I don't. There are tarantula mites and the frogs grow fat eating these. If they didn't, the mites would eat the spider's eggs. The spider could eat the frogs but it doesn't. This is a choice, but one more easily made without regret because of how the frogs secrete a toxin that makes their skin taste vile to a spider. They love each other, frog and tarantula, like people who need each other do.

Like a tarantula maybe, or a frog, or a mite, it is hard to see your place in the system from within it. Like you I bring my legal pad to the working lunches, file the report, explain to a man how I make less than him despite having accomplished more, explain to another I am neither complimented nor amused to be called a girl, notice the women who are not white like me making less than all of us, remember money is a symbol as much as a cut flower or a ring. I try to figure out how to take power and give up power at the same time, and love, too, somewhere in this.

Of course none of us is a frog and none a spider. None of what we do is eggs or mites or nest. They are not symbols, only themselves. In that way too we are like them.

You and I were talking of dresses across five hundred miles, scrolling pictures of this blue or that one, while my child, your nibling, our dear, pulled a frog from every stoop and bush in the town square. This happens sometimes—there are a few days each season when all the young of a particular species emerge leaping at once. It is called a bloom and in general, humans miss it, the slick abundance often too small or vast, time fleeting, our eyes on door handles and not the broken places in concrete.

But sometimes we don't miss the moment, we are there and we see it. As I have seen over and again on this wedding day, like frog upon frog, how tenderly John can look at you. Outside it is another flood year. Frogs are the uncountable millions, birds in decline by a third this decade alone. There are lifetimes in those looks. I wonder who else at this banquet hates themselves, their dress, their flute of champagne for how their comfort is tied to the picture in this morning's news or yesterday's of someone's weeping child. Perhaps no one else.

The tarantula's name can be translated as "the velvet brush." Though they live in burrows in the ground, they still weave silken webs for mating. I find it strange, the occasions that bring us together, the ones that do not. But the way you sometimes reach for his hand, that is easy to understand.

Sister, the truth is that I will love you all our lives. It may be that you have taken his name—you know I wished you wouldn't because you told me to shut up about it and I will presently—but always no matter what, you are one of us and I am one of you. All around frogs are feasting, spiders are hatching, there are children out there laughing to hold them all, tiny treasures, in their cupped palms, let us not miss the moment.

LINES ABOUT THE MOON

In time the wild mustard brittles back to a stem of moons, each one thick with seed.

The moon of a distant lamp glows outside of everything.

What I miss most is how the moonflowers would unfurl in the falling light.

The shell of a horseshoe crab in the sunlit water is more like a moon than not.

Horseshoe crabs keep gardens of algae, periwinkles, and barnacles on their backs. They hardly notice they are becoming a living island unless the algae grows over the eye on their neck that is good for watching the moon.

They are so sensitive to light they bury themselves in the sand and wait for moonrise to resume their scuttling.

Once upon a time horseshoe crabs were so abundant the salt marshes were thick with their eggs, which are translucent orbs cradling a gelatinous yellow shelled being making itself from shadows like a face on the moon.

Red knots, migrating twice a year from the north pole to the south and back again, pause here to feast. Or they once did. Hungry and fading, they navigate the earth on the memory of all those eggs spilling across the briny grasses. The moon pulls at them, her tiniest tremors their compass.

What is wind? How long does the past last? When does the circle of forever come back around? The moon bends the water to hold the pebble of its eye.

THRESHOLDS

A few years ago, two explorers made the last summer hike to the north pole. So much ice had melted they had to wear wet suits and ford rivers of glacial meltwaters, pulling their sled of gear behind like a raft. The next year and every year since, you can only make the journey by boat, which is something else entirely.

Back home in Mexico City, Perla makes installations. In her most recent she turned an art gallery into a rock field. The floor was covered in small stones, but she also rolled in massive boulders to hold the space. In pictures from her portfolio you can see adults leaning against the cool black boulders while children sit in the pebbles running handfuls through their fingers and watching how they fall.

She was the eldest of us, and when a covid outbreak passed through the ship became the most ill of anyone. When she was finally well enough to walk on deck, someone had to hold firmly to her elbow so the wind would not knock her back. I had to remind myself she was a sculptor who wielded mountains.

Unable to carry herself very far, while the rest of us hiked the glacier, she gathered tern feathers and a little of the bright blue fishing net strands we'd find clumped up on all the beaches. She roped them together into a miniature doorway she'd balance on a hunk of washed-up ice. Then she'd wait for some glimmer of light to pass through and take a picture.

At dinner after the long hike up the back of a fast-melting glacier she asked me for my phone and insisted I describe every picture I'd taken. I liked sitting with her because I was still bleeding a little every day and though I didn't want to talk about it, it felt less frightening to be near one of the only other people on the boat who'd ever been pregnant.

Where the ice had melted there was a vast rock field entirely made of petrified wood. Any boulder you might sit on to catch your breath you soon realized was a huge and ancient tree stump. Everywhere boughs had become marble-smooth stones, on one side you could run your thumb along polished bark, on the other the reddish gleam of heartwood, coursing veins that had carried sap to and from the roots. I repeated to Perla what the geologist among us had told me—during the Triassic all this land had been a tropical forest at the equator. As tectonic plates shifted these islands north, the ice pressed and pressed those trees into something else entirely.

Her favorite of my pictures was the one I took at the place where the river of melting ice slowed its torrent into a wide, smooth delta passing into the sea. Long strands of algae drifted a lovely green across the glittering sand.

There is grief and fear of the grief to come and the smallest hope things could be different. The algae was beautiful and also another sign of a place at the beginning and end of itself.

In my pocket I had four hunks of petrified wood I had collected—one for Brian, one for his mother who is always picking up some bit of quartz that has caught her eye, one for my kid, and one I felt guilty for taking, as it was no gift, just a greedy hunger to fill my pockets with as much of this beauty as I could carry. Perla said she could not accept something so precious, so as we hugged goodnight, I slipped it in the pocket of the sweater that hung so loose now around her shoulders.

After twenty days without cell service or Wi-Fi, we docked. One of the guides drove me straight to a clinic where two kind Norwegian women, bashful about their English, turn the ultrasound screen toward me and say, "Look! Two heartbeats!" One twin is too small, precariously small. I should see a specialist when I get home. But as I start to fret the doctor looks me in the eye and says firmly, "But today there are two heartbeats."

I stop at the café across from the clinic and find Perla eating a piece of lingonberry pie she says is too much for her. She points to the chair beside her and hands me a fork. As we eat, I tell her this secret I have been carrying for so long like a stone in my pocket.

"Today there are two heartbeats."

On Love, Dear Friend, I Can't Think About It Without Thinking a Minute About You

There are a lot of ways to understand the world, but I prefer fungi, which are connected to and connecting everything that grows. No more than filaments to the human eye, almost imperceptible hums beneath the soil, on occasion exploding forth in their brand of orgasm, a poison-delicious red sporocarp or a deep orange oozing. Every gust of wind is a blush of spores loosed across the forest.

I heard that a tree fell on your house and though you grieve the tree, you are glad to at least be thinking about something else for a change. Neighbors in my old life had a hundred-year oak with a knot that began as a lost limb, then a scar, but grew over decades into a heart-shaped hole children fed marbles and little plastic horses. Squirrels packed the opening every autumn with its own acorns.

When my own walnut was lightning struck down the middle, I thought I would watch it die slow, woodpeckered, the beetles, then fungus. But the rent barkened over, one half of the tree stayed tall, the other arced a bridge to the ground. A new forest of saplings rose up from the fire-scarred back of the curving bough.

The owners of the house with the heart tree were almost as old as their oak and tender. Though they had the tree cut down when it threatened their roof, they left the heart stump. A sweet gesture, but without any green for shade, it felt like walking past a grave.

I returned after some years away to visit that neighborhood and saw the wife without her husband for the first time. They used to walk every evening to the end of the block and back, no further than that, his fingers holding her elbow for balance. I realize I've never seen her alone before and this probably meant he had passed. I whizzed by on my bicycle. She smiled and I knew she was not thinking of her husband just then.

We aren't the same people we were. The fungi are like hair and when your hair is down the wind carries it. This bike has a little bell to ring as you pass her by.

THE DAUGHTERS

The phasmids, of the order Phasmatodea, are also called ghost insects. I know them better as walking sticks, for their clever way of hiding in plain sight. Their eggs look like small black seeds. Their thin eyes, which burn in the daylight, grow with them from their first instar in the leaves through a fully formed adult life in the night, where they see as clear as day.

A walking stick once hung dangling from my finger. I was a child and did not know what she was or what she was becoming.

They can lay eggs without mating, producing a generation of nymphs just like their mother. In this way they are like certain plants—strawberries, for example, which produce both runners and seeds.

There will be an eclipse this afternoon. The phasmids will wake confused and stir the brown leaves as egrets rise up from the marsh grasses in the far field and circle each other for those few inexplicable minutes. It is only a coincidence—my feelings and this sky.

My neighbor died yesterday. She was not my grandmother, it only felt that way sometimes, as if she was the neighborhood's grandmother. I would sit at her table, drinking from her mother's teacup and watch as she folded and unfolded all the little drawings my child and her child, her grandchildren and other people's grandchildren ever made for her. Each one she would hold up and say, "Isn't it beautiful?" as I sipped.

Sometimes she would tell me riddles she remembered her mother telling her back in Saint Petersburg when she was a little girl. I would try to help translate. Though she worked as a chemist when her memory was more clear, she loved words like a poet and lingered over their connotations. We have a hard time getting this one right. A cabbage is one thousand vestments? A cabbage is one thousand shirts? It's not supposed to be sacred or silly, it's supposed to feel like your mother has bundled you up to go out in the snow.

Undershirt, overshirt, blouse, and sweater.

Crisp outside, a warm heart in the pot.

Ghost Song

Little lullaby of how it's okay, little okay of how it's not, little rhyme of too much wishing, little wish for so much more, little life of risks and gambits, little wondering what it's for, little for of all this sun on all this snow, little hour when someone was born and lived awhile. Little while, little day, little cries, little cardinal on the fence, little song crisp and piercing through the air, every breath anyone ever took, we breathe it in, little falling asleep sigh, we breathe it in again.

The Primaeval Ocean

One of the first symbioses was the one between plants and animals via this thing we call air. Before the invention of the CO_2 - O_2 exchange cycle, there was the first mass extinction. Plants were choking on their own abundance as the too muchness of all their breathing out and out and out turned the atmosphere into nothing but oxygen they had no use for, with carbon dioxide nowhere to be found.

Sometimes I go to huge university libraries and try to get lost. I wander up and down the rows with my finger running along the spines, waiting for something to happen.

This is how I found myself trying to learn how to read fragmented papyri from an ancient Egyptian text you might call *On the Primaeval Ocean*, though it has been catalogued as the Carlsberg Papyri V. An epic cosmology from Northern Egypt, it has been divided, discarded as rubbish, forgotten in a drawer in a basement, and disfigured by salts taken up in the roots of the papyrus plant effloresced to crystals within the very fibers of the paper. The scroll is embrittled, fractured, pockmarked by insect tunnels, spackled by fungus. Illustrated by a copper-based pigment, the ink darkened to brown and black. In and around the pigment area the ink burns through the papyrus. Before the scroll was unrolled it was used as a nest by mice.

In this work something akin to the idea of God is called the Primaeval Ocean. That divinity begins to call itself across its own waves, with each new word emanating forth as more particularized divinities—the ocean calls forth gods of lightness and darkness, earth and sky. Then come the bird-headed and crocodile-headed gods, a lotus, a bull, a cow, papyrus reeds, a child.

I don't think about God much anymore, but when I do, I'm partial to the story about the breath of life moving across the waters.

The emergence of that green spear of papyrus on the marshy earth is an important moment in the text because these are the plants that will become the paper the world is written on. When translating it is not always clear whether to say "the plant" or "field." Just as it is not always clear when we are ourselves and when we are each other.

Another of the very first symbioses was the one that would become the mitochondria in our cells. Parasitic bacteria in plant cells evolved to feed their hosts as their hosts fed them, because you can only have so much death and destruction before life must emerge somehow again. This theory was developed and advanced, at first in the face of a great deal of ridicule in the scientific community, by Lynn Margulis.

Because I am a poet, not a scientist, I am convinced it is relevant that while Margulis was studying the nature of entanglements within entanglements that constitute the essence of our cellular chemistry, she was in a failing marriage to Carl Sagan. Carl Sagan, the beloved pop culture icon and scientist of the cosmos, who said, "Look again at that dot. That's here. That's home. That's us. On it everyone you love, everyone you know, everyone you ever heard of . . . every saint and sinner in the history of our species lived there—on a mote of dust suspended in a sunbeam."

He made a recording of his research assistant's beating heart when they were having an affair during his second marriage. And that heartbeat is on the Golden Record careening through space on Voyager 1 along with bars from *The Rite of Spring*. He wanted the aliens to know something about how we love. But not everything, because he did not record his own heart, beating betrayal and reckless foolishness and delusions with all its might. He was so in love, he could imagine hers was the sound of something pure. Or maybe he liked the idea of himself being loved lasting for a billion years more than the idea of his own love in return lasting forever.

I don't really think ill of Carl Sagan. People fall in and out of love all the time. They hurt each other too. I have. I simply want you to remember every time you hear what Carl Sagan said about this little blue dot that it was Lynn Margulis who realized the essence of our being is not a mutually assured destruction, but rather, the way we come back to each other after.

HOME

WINDOW
The sky is in, the sky is out.
One way the whole world fits
in a box, the other and your eye
becomes a field of blue.

DOOR
Always reaching to take your hand,
she gives a little twirl as you swing her.
A heart breaks closed with a click.

I prefer to know the answer to a riddle before it begins, so I can focus on the riddler's peculiar way of seeing. The way their little poems first estrange us, then bring us back to the known world.

When Alice and their friends were little, it was so easy to amaze them. I'd put an apple on the table: "Little red house, with a chimney on top," I'd say. Then cut it in half and hold up the white flesh with its perfect pentagon of seeds at the center. "And a star inside."

When the kids were little it was so easy to amaze myself. It was as if I too had never seen into an apple before. Even now I can't crack an egg without remembering, "This is a house with a sun inside."

As they got older, the riddles I had to offer grew more complicated. In a drop of water, magnified, we found diatoms, tiny plants who live in houses made of glass. Glass—technically

I mean silicate shells that grow in intricate patterns around the soft green and gold parts of their bodies. It's a fun little game to name them like clouds—double snowflake, whorl of screw, teeth of a key. One of the riddles of these microscopic algae is that they do not die, only divide in two. They do this again. They do this again. They do this for seven generations, growing smaller and smaller. And then the immortal diatoms burst soft and stretchy from their glass and float, wide as a beginning, back to the surface of the water to once more split and split and continue becoming.

Sometimes I feel the wind has no home. Or I am become part of the wind that has no home. Or a child has been swept into the homelessness of the wind. Squirrel Nutkin said of smoke, "A house full, a hole full! And you cannot gather a bowl full!" Other answers to that riddle are soul, spirit, the breath of life.

Of course the diatoms die—all living things do. The art of the riddle is to make something impossible briefly, beautifully true.

> Who can remember being inside
> their mother? Sometimes the wind
> is frightening. Sometimes we wonder
> how we've been away so long.

Bibliography

AN AUBADE IS A MOURNING SONG

Peralta, Eyder. "Sudan, World's Last Male Northern White Rhino, Dies." *All Things Considered*, National Public Radio, March 20, 2018. https://www.npr.org/sections/parallels/2018/03/20/591075801.

Stanton, M. L., and T. P. Young. "Thorny Relationships." *Natural History* 108, no. 9 (1999): 28–31.

Wikipedia. "List of Endangered Species in Missouri." Last modified July 23, 2023, at 13:47 (UTC). https://en.wikipedia.org/wiki/List_of_endangered_species_in_Missouri.

CLOSE

Colvard, Mary, Tom Vawter, Tim Downs, Veronica Dunham, Meg Maisch, and Jeanne Raish. "You've Got a Lot of Galls!" Teacher guide for lab investigation. Cornell Institute for Biology Teachers, 1998. Revised during CIBT Alumni Workshop, Summer 2013.

THE OWLS

Fischer, Adelheid. "Hope and the Thing with Feathers." *Zygote Quarterly* 1, no. 22 (2018): 93–107.

Spies, A. Thomas, Jonathan W. Long, Susan Charnley, et al. "Twenty-Five Years of the Northwest Forest Plan: What Have We Learned?" *Frontiers in Ecology and the Environment* 17, no. 9 (2019): 511–20.

CAIRNS

Carson, Rachel. *The Edge of the Sea*. Houghton Mifflin, 1955. Reprint, Mariner Books, 1998.

Cooney, Margaret, and Violet Sage Walker. "The Chumash Heritage National Marine Sanctuary: An Interview with Violet Sage Walker." *Parks Stewardship Forum* 38, no. 2 (2022): 317–24.

Liboiron, Max. *Pollution Is Colonialism*. Duke University Press, 2021.

ARCHIVES AT THE END OF THE WORLD

Quante, Heidi, and Alicia Escott. *Bureau of Linguistical Reality*. Accessed May 1, 2024. https://bureauoflinguisticalreality.com.

Schneider-Mayerson, Matthew, and Brent Ryan Bellamy, eds. *An Ecotopian Lexicon*. University of Minnesota Press, 2019.

HAVING HAD HAPPENED

Kaprow, Allan. *Essays on the Blurring of Art and Life*. Edited by Jeff Kelley. University of California Press, 2003.

THE HARD PROBLEM

Chalmers, David. "Facing Up to the Problem of Consciousness." *Journal of Consciousness Studies* 2, no. 3 (1995): 200–19.

Moseley, Edwin Lincoln. *Milk Sickness Caused by White Snakeroot*. Ohio Academy of Science; the author, 1941.

Revonsuo, Antti, and James Newman. "Binding and Consciousness." *Consciousness and Cognition* 8, no. 2 (1999): 123–27.

THE SINGULAR SELF

Aldini, Giovanni. "An Account of the Late Improvements in Galvanism, with a series of Curious and Interesting Experiments Performed before the Commissioners of the French National Institute, and Repeated Lately in the Anatomical Theaters of London by John Aldini, to which is added, an Appendix, containing the author's experiments on the body of a malefactor Executed at Newgate. &c. &c. Illustrated with engravings." London, 1803. *The Public Domain Review*, August 2, 2011. https://publicdomainreview.org/collection/an-account-of-the-late-improvements-in-galvanism-1803.

Wilson, Eric G. "Matter and Spirit in the Age of Animal Magnetism." *Philosophy and Literature* 30, no. 2 (2006): 329–45.

BREAKING

Buckeridge, John. "Of Trees, Geese and Cirripedes: Man's Quest for Understanding." *Integrative Zoology* 6, no. 1 (2011): 3–12.

Hepburn, R. W. *"Wonder" and Other Essays: Eight Studies in Aesthetics and Neighbouring Fields*. Edinburgh University Press, 1984.

SILENCE

Cypess, Rebecca. "'It Would Be Without Error': Automated Technology and the Pursuit of Correct Performance in the French Enlightenment." *Journal of the Royal Musical Association* 142, no. 1 (2017): 1–29.

Guiley, Rosemary Ellen. "Caim (Caym, Camio)." In *The Encyclopedia of Demons and Demonology*. Facts on File, 2009.

THINKING IS A KIND OF FEELING . . .

Brunner, Bernd. "Bringing the Ocean Home." *Public Domain Review*, June 21, 2018. https://publicdomainreview.org/essay/bringing-the-ocean-home.

Gosse, Philip Henry. *The Aquarium: An Unveiling of the Wonders of the Deep Sea*. London, 1856. https://archive.org/details/b28121211.

THINGS THAT REPEAT THEMSELVES

Bell, Catherine. *Ritual Theory, Ritual Practice*. Oxford University Press, 1992. Reprinted with new forward by Diane Jonte-Pace. Oxford University Press, 2009.

Hettenhausen, Christian, Juan Li, Huifu Zhuang, et al. "Stem Parasitic Plant *Cuscuta australis* (Dodder) Transfers Herbivory-Induced Signals Among Plants." *Proceedings of the National Academy of Sciences of the United States of America* 114, no. 32 (2017): E6703–9.

NO. 65, THE HUMANS ARE LOST TO MADNESS . . .

Eidinow, Esther. "Madness." In *The Oxford Companion to Classical Civilization*, edited by Simon Hornblower and Antony Spawforth. 2nd ed. Oxford University Press, 2014.

Gates, Alexander E., and Robert P. Blauvelt. "Doe Run Smelter: Herculaneum, Missouri 2001 Air Pollution." In *Encyclopedia of Pollution*, vol. 1. Facts on File, 2011.

Schulz, Andrew. *Goya's* Caprichos*: Aesthetics, Perception, and the Body*. Cambridge University Press, 2005.

HOMESTEADS

Fraser, Caroline. *Prairie Fires: The American Dreams of Laura Ingalls Wilder*. Picador, 2018.

Hernandez, Jessica. *Fresh Banana Leaves: Healing Indigenous Landscapes Through Indigenous Science*. North Atlantic Books, 2022.

Jefferson, Thomas. "To Madame de Tessé, *26 October*." In *The Papers of Thomas Jefferson, Volume 47: 6 July to 19 November 1805*, edited by James P. McClure. Princeton University Press, 2023.

Pollan, Michael. *The Botany of Desire: A Plant's-Eye View of the World*. Bloomsbury, 2003.

Zitkala-Ša. "Four Autobiographical Narratives (1900–1902)." In *Classic American Autobiographies*, edited by William L. Andrews. Signet Classics, 2014.

ZUGUNRUHE

Allaby, Michael. "Zugunruhe." *A Dictionary of Zoology*. 4th ed. Oxford University Press, 2014.

Soniak, Matt. "How Does a Cowbird Lean to Be a Cowbird?" *Audubon* (news blog). Feb. 25, 2016. https://www.audubon.org/news/how-does-cowbird-learn-be-cowbird.

THE COMPLEX BIOLOGICAL ENTITY KNOWN AS SKY

Convention on the Prohibition of Military or Any Other Hostile Use of Environmental Modification Techniques. Signed in Geneva May 18, 1977. Entered into force October 5, 1978. Bureau of International Security and Nonproliferation. Archived at the US Department of State website, January 20, 2009–January 20, 2017. https://2009-2017.state.gov/t/isn/4783.htm.

Pollitzer, Anita. *A Woman on Paper: Georgia O'Keeffe*. Simon & Schuster, 1988.

Šantl-Temkiv, Tina, Pierre Amato, Emilio O. Casamayor, Patrick K. H. Lee, and Stephen B. Pointing. "Microbial Ecology of the Atmosphere." *FEMS Microbiology Reviews* 46, no. 4 (2022): fuac009. https://doi.org/10.1093/femsre/fuac009.

Sturluson, Snorri. *Edda. Skáldskaparmál.* Edited by Anthony Faulkes. Viking Society for Northern Research; University College London, 1998.

NOWHERE ELSE

Mauna Kea Education and Awareness. "Mauna Kea Facts." Accessed May 26, 2025. https://www.mkea.info/protectmaunakea-1.

Oliveira, Katrina-Ann R. Kapāʻanaokalāokeola Nākoa, and Erin Kahunawaikaʻala Wright, eds. *Kanaka ʻŌiwi Methodologies: Moʻolelo and Metaphor*. University of Hawaiʻi Press, 2016.

A GREEN BEJEWELMENT

Curran, Mike. "Tracking Change and Growth at Crosby Farm." Mississippi National River and Recreation Area, National Park Service. Accessed May 26, 2025. https://www.nps.gov/articles/000/tracking-change-and-growth-at-crosby-farm.htm.

Kimmerer, Robin Wall. *Braiding Sweetgrass*. Milkweed Editions, 2013.

LECTURE NOTES ON LITERATURE AND EMPATHY

Sharif, Solmaz. *Customs*. Graywolf, 2022.

Stein, Edith. *On the Problem of Empathy*. Translated by Waltraut Stein. ICS Publications, 1989.

ONSLAUGHTS

Gleditsch, Jason M., and Tomás A. Carlo. "Fruit Quantity of Invasive Shrubs Predicts the Abundance of Common Native Avian Frugivores in Central Pennsylvania." *Diversity and Distributions* 17, no. 2 (2011): 244–53.

Kettle, W. Dean, Paul M. Rich, Kelly Kindscher, Galen L. Pittman, and Pinde Fu. "Land-Use History in Ecosystem Restoration: A 40-Year Study in the Prairie-Forest Ecotone." *Restoration Ecology* 8, no. 3 (2000): 307–17.

Kimmerer, Robin Wall. *Braiding Sweetgrass*. Milkweed Editions, 2013.

PORCUPINE GRASS, GREEN NEEDLE . . .

Geniusz, Mary Siisip. *Plants Have So Much to Give Us, All We Have to Do Is Ask: Anishinaabe Botanical Teachings*. Edited by Wendy Makoons Geniusz. University of Minnesota Press, 2015.

Kimmerer, Robin Wall. *Braiding Sweetgrass*. Milkweed Editions, 2013.

McKittrick, Katherine. *Dear Science and Other Stories*. Duke University Press, 2021.

Sharpe, Christina. "Dionne Brand's *A Map to the Door of No Return* at 20: A Gathering." *TOPIA: Canadian Journal of Cultural Studies* 46, no. 1 (2023): 1–6.

ON THE GREEN LINE

Holzer, Jenny. *Retro*. Text by Cary Levine. Skarstedt, 2011. Exhibition catalog.

Sheldrake, Merlin. *Entangled Life: How Fungi Make Our Worlds, Change Our Minds and Shape Our Futures*. Illus. ed. Random House, 2023.

Tsing, Anna Lowenhaupt. *The Mushroom at the End of the World: On the Possibility of Life in Capitalist Ruins*. Princeton University Press, 2015.

IN THE DISTANCE A PHAINOPEPLA FLIES . . .

Columbia Daily Tribune. "Library changes signs prohibiting guns." Feb. 17, 2017.

Elliott, Caroline M., Aaron J. DeLonay, Kimberly A. Chojnacki, and Robert B. Jacobson. "Characterization of Pallid Sturgeon (*Scaphirhynchus albus*) Spawning Habitat in the Lower Missouri River." *Journal of Applied Ichthyology* 36, no. 1 (2020): 25–38.

Kropotkin, Peter. *Mutual Aid: A Factor of Evolution*. 1st Canadian ed. Black Rose Books, 1989.

Nature Conservancy. "Verde River, Arizona." Places We Protect. Accessed May 1, 2023. https://www.nature.org/en-us/get-involved/how-to-help/places-we-protect/verde-river.

Rogers, Jenny. "Barley Dreams: An Arizona town gambles on beer to save water." *Nature Conservancy*, Spring 2020. Posted online February 29, 2020. https://www.nature.org/en-us/magazine/magazine-articles/barley-dreams.

WHAT IS PAST

Althoff, David M. "Specialization in the Yucca–Yucca Moth Obligate Pollination Mutualism: A Role for Antagonism?" *American Journal of Botany* 103, no. 10 (2016): 1803–09.

National Park Service. "Not Just the Peanut Man." George Washington Carver National Monument. Last updated May 1, 2025. https://www.nps.gov/gwca/index.htm.

Yusoff, Kathryn. *A Billion Black Anthropocenes or None*. University of Minnesota Press, 2018.

ALLEYS

Cohen, Meagan Leah, Ekaterina Vadimovna Mashanova, Nicholas Matthew Rosen, and William Soto. "Adaptation to Temperature Stress by *Vibrio fischeri* Facilitates This Microbe's Symbiosis with the Hawaiian Bobtail Squid (*Euprymna scolopes*)." *Evolution* 73, no. 9 (2019): 1885–97.

ON ERROR

Barber, Richard, trans. *Bestiary: Being an English Version of the Bodleian Library, Oxford, MS Bodley 764*. Boydell Press, 1999.

Pleasonton, A. J. *The Influence of the Blue Ray of the Sunlight and of the Blue Colour of the Sky*. Philadelphia, 1877.

AFTER

McMahon, William J., and Neil S. Davies. "Evolution of Alluvial Mudrock Forced by Early Land Plants." *Science* 359, no. 6379 (2018): 1022–24.

Spribille, Toby, Philipp Resl, Danuel E. Stanton, and Gulnara Tagirdzhanova. "Evolutionary Biology of Lichen Symbioses." *New Phytologist* 234, no. 5 (2022): 1566–82.

THE HISTORY OF DISREPAIR

Kiser, Joy M. *America's Other Audubon*. With illustrations by Genevieve Jones (1847–1879). Princeton Architectural Press, 2012.

AGAINST AN APOCALYPTIC VISION

Stewart, Susan. *The Ruins Lesson: Meaning and Material in Western Culture*. University of Chicago Press, 2021.

THE SPACE BETWEEN US

Banerjee, Anirban, Soumabrota Poddar, Subha Manna, and Samar Kumar Saha. "Mutualistic Association of Rotifer *Philodina roseola* with the Branchiuran Fish Ectoparasite *Argulus bengalensis* at Its Embryonic Stage." *Biology Letters* 12, no. 3 (2016): 20151043. https://doi.org/10.1098/rsbl.2015.1043.

Leeuwenhoek, Antoni van. *The Collected Letters of Antoni van Leeuwenhoek*. Edited and annotated by a Committee of Dutch Scientists. 19 vols. Swets and Zeitlinger, 1939. Reprint, CRC Press, 2021.

AGAINST MORALS OF THE STORY . . .

Maruyama, Munetoshi, and Joseph Parker. "Deep-Time Convergence in Rove Beetle Symbionts of Army Ants." *Current Biology* 27, no. 6 (2017): 920–26.

MERMAIDS

DeVries, P. J. "Enhancement of Symbioses Between Butterfly Caterpillars and Ants by Vibrational Communication." *Science* 248, no. 4959 (1990): 1104–06.

Gegenbauer, Christian, Veronika E. Mayer, Gerhard Zotz, and Andreas Richter. "Uptake of Ant-Derived Nitrogen in the Myrmecophytic Orchid *Caularthron bilamellatum*." *Annals of Botany* 110, no. 4 (2012): 757–66.

STRANGERS

Leong, Felicia Wei Shan, Weng Ngai Lam, and Hugh Tiang Wah Tan. "A Dipteran Larva–Pitcher Plant Digestive Mutualism Is Dependent on Prey Resource Digestibility." *Oecologia* 188, no. 3 (2018): 813–20.

Schöner, Michael G., Caroline R. Schöner, Rebecca Ermisch, et al. "Stabilization of a Bat–Pitcher Plant Mutualism." *Scientific Reports* 7, no. 1 (2017): 13170. https://doi.org/10.1038/s41598-017-13535-5.

A DEFINITION OF LONGING

Flaherty, David. "Chartreuse, the Ancient French Liqueur, Makes a Comeback." *Nation's Restaurant News*, June 22, 2021. https://www.nrn.com/beverage-trends/chartreuse-the-ancient-french-liqueur-makes-a-comeback.

Miller, Brooke L. W. "Sexual Conflict and Partner Manipulation in the Banana Slug, *Ariolimax dolichophallus*." PhD diss., University of California, Santa Cruz, 2007. ProQuest (304882120).

Plato. *Plato: Complete Works*. Edited, with notes and introduction, by John M. Cooper. Hackett, 1997.

Richter, Klaus Otto. "The Foraging Ecology of the Banana Slug *Ariolimax columbianus*, Gould (Arionidae)." PhD diss., University of Washington, 1976. ProQuest (7718410).

A KINDNESS OF SPARROWS

Kostuch, Lucyna, Beata Wojciechowska, and Sylwia Konarska-Zimnicka. "Ancient and Medieval Animals and Self-Recognition: Observations from Early European Sources." *Early Science and Medicine* 24, no. 2 (2019): 117–41.

Rowland, Beryl. *Birds with Human Souls: A Guide to Bird Symbolism*. University of Tennessee Press, 1978.

LONELINESS

Barthelemy, Hélène, Ellen Dorrepaal, and Johan Olofsson. "Defoliation of a Grass Is Mediated by the Positive Effect of Dung Deposition, Moss Removal and Enhanced Soil Nutrient Contents: Results from a Reindeer Grazing Simulation Experiment." *Oikos* 128, no. 10 (2019): 1515–24.

Dinneen, James. "Invasion of Jellyfish Could Disrupt Arctic Ecosystems." *New Scientist* 262, no. 3492 (2024): 19.

Giggs, Rebecca. *Fathoms: The World in the Whale*. Simon & Schuster, 2020.

EVERYTHING IS GOING TO BE ALRIGHT

Yong, Ed. "Cicadas Have an Existential Problem." *Atlantic*, May 5, 2021. https://www.theatlantic.com/science/archive/2021/05/cicada-brood-x-bacteria-chaos/618808.

ON THE OTHER SIDE OF ENDING, THERE IS

Bauman, Jenise M., Sarah Francino, and Amy Santas. "Interactions Between Ectomycorrhizal Fungi and Chestnut Blight (*Cryphonectria parasitica*) on American Chestnut (*Castanea dentata*) Used in Coal Mine Restoration." *AIMS Microbiology* 4, no. 1 (2018): 104–22.

Kane, Jeffrey M., J. Morgan Varner, Michael C. Stambaugh, and Michael R. Saunders. "Reconsidering the Fire Ecology of the Iconic American Chestnut." *Ecosphere* 11, no. 10 (2020): e03267. https://doi.org/10.1002/ecs2.3267.

ʻŪHINI NĒNĒ PELE

Price, Michael. "For These Intrepid Crickets, Lava Is Home Sweet Home." *Science* 363, no. 6433 (2019): 1262.

THE NEST, THE SEED, THE EGG, THE SPIRAL

Dunn, Derek W. "Stability in Fig Tree–Fig Wasp Mutualisms: How to Be a Cooperative Fig Wasp." *Biological Journal of the Linnean Society* 130, no. 1 (2020): 1–17.

HOW THE MUSSEL, HOW THE FISH . . .

Demi. *The Stonecutter*. Crown, 1995.

Ries, Patricia, Nathan R. De Jager, Steve J. Zigler, and Teresa J. Newton. "Spatial Patterns of Native Freshwater Mussels in the Upper Mississippi River." *Freshwater Science* 35, no. 3 (2016): 934–47.

Wisniewski, Jason M., Katherine D. Bockrath, John P. Wares, Andrea K. Fritts, and Matthew J. Hill. "The Mussel–Fish Relationship: A Potential New Twist in North America?" *Transactions of the American Fisheries Society* 142, no. 3 (2013): 642–48.

THE BARRENS

Galloway, A. W. E., S. A. Gravem, J. N. Kobelt, et al. "Sunflower Sea Star Predation on Urchins Can Facilitate Kelp Forest Recovery." *Proceedings of the Royal Society B: Biological Sciences* 290, no. 1993 (2023): 20221897. https://doi.org/10.1098/rspb.2022.1897.

Lafferty, Kevin D., and Thomas H. Suchanek. "Revisiting Paine's 1966 Sea Star Removal Experiment, the Most-Cited Empirical Article in the *American Naturalist*." *American Naturalist* 188, no. 4 (2016): 365–78.

Paine, Robert T. "Food Web Complexity and Species Diversity." *American Naturalist* 100, no. 910 (1966): 65–75.

Rose, Deborah Bird, Thom van Dooren, and Matthew Chrulew, eds. *Extinction Studies: Stories of Time, Death, and Generations*. Columbia University Press, 2017.

Smith, Joshua G., Joseph Tomoleoni, Michelle Staedler, Sophia Lyon, Jessica Fujii, and M. Tim Tinker. "Behavioral Responses Across a Mosaic of Ecosystem States Restructure a Sea Otter–Urchin Trophic Cascade." *Proceedings of the National Academy of Sciences (PNAS)* 118, no. 11 (2021): e2012493118. https://doi.org/10.1073/pnas.2012493118.

Yodzis, Peter. "Diffuse Effects in Food Webs." *Ecology* 81, no. 1 (2000): 261–66.

LITTLE WHITE-WINGED MOTHS . . .

Svensson, Glenn P., Olle Pellmyr, and Robert Raguso. "Pollinator Attraction to Volatiles from Virgin and Pollinated Host Flowers in a Yucca/Moth Obligate Mutualism." *Oikos* 120, no. 10 (2011): 1577–83.

UMWELTEN

Bugs Below Zero. *Bugs Below Zero: Discovering Winter Aquatic Insects in Minnesota*. University of Minnesota. Accessed February 5, 2024. https://www.bugsbelowzero.com.

Fabre, Jean-Henri. *The Passionate Observer: Writings from the World of Nature*. Edited by Linda Davis. Chronicle Books, 1998.

Uexküll, Jakob von. *A Foray into the Worlds of Animals and Humans: With A Theory of Meaning*. Translated by Joseph D. O'Neil. University of Minnesota Press, 2010.

EPITHALAMIUMS ARE A BULLSHIT POETIC FORM . . .

Csakany, Jolene Jeana. "Some Aspects of the Relationship Between the Peruvian Microhylid Frog, *Chiasmocleis ventrimaculata*, and a Theraphosid Spider, *Pamphobetus* Sp." Master's thesis, State University of New York College of Environmental Science and Forestry, 2003. ProQuest (1413905).

LINES ABOUT THE MOON

Nixon, Eli. *Bloodtide: A New Holiday in Homage to Horseshoe Crabs.* The 3rd Thing, 2021.

THRESHOLDS

Clynes, Tom. "Measuring the End of the World: Explorers Hike to the North Pole to Figure Out How Fast Arctic Ice Is Melting." *Popular Science* 274, no. 2 (2009): 28–29.

Pott, Christian, Johan van der Burgh, and Johanna H. A. van Konijnenburg-van Cittert. "New Ginkgophytes from the Upper Triassic–Lower Cretaceous of Spitsbergen and Edgeøya (Svalbard, Arctic Norway): The History of Ginkgoales on Svalbard." Edited by Patrick S. Herendeen. *International Journal of Plant Sciences* 177, no. 2 (2016): 175–97.

THE DAUGHTERS

O'Hanlon, James C., Braxton R. Jones, and Matthew W. Bulbert. "The Dynamic Eggs of the Phasmatodea and Their Apparent Convergence with Plants." *Die Naturwissenschaften* 107, no. 4 (2020): 34.

THE PRIMAEVAL OCEAN

Margulis, Lynn. *Symbiotic Planet: A New Look at Evolution.* Basic Books, 1998.

Sagan, Carl. *The Pale Blue Dot: Short Recording.* Audio. Retrieved from the Library of Congress, February 14, 2025. https://www.loc.gov/item/cosmos000110.

Smart, Matthew S., Gabriel Filippelli, William P. Gilhooly III, et al. "The Expansion of Land Plants during the Late Devonian Contributed to the Marine Mass Extinction." *Communications Earth & Environment* 4, no. 1 (2023): 449. https://doi.org/10.1038/s43247-023-01087-8.

Smith, Mark. *On the Primaeval Ocean: The Carlsberg Papyri 5*. The Carsten Niebuhr Institute of Near Eastern Studies; Musem Tusculanum Press; The Carlsberg Papyri, 2002.

HOME

Potter, Beatrix. *The Tale of Squirrel Nutkin*. Grolier, 1960. Originally published in 1903 by Frederick Warne & Co.

Spaulding, Sarah A., Marina G. Potapova, Ian W. Bishop, et al. *Diatoms.org: Supporting Taxonomists, Connecting Communities* (website). *Diatom Research* 36, no. 4 (2021): 291–304. https://doi.org/10.1080/0269249X.2021.2006790.

ACKNOWLEDGMENTS

My family grew in many ways as I wrote this book. Polina, Paul, Iko, Leo, and Gaga introduced me to the idea of mutualism in all its forms. Doug, Nicole, Elijah, and Khalilah opened the world back up to us. My dear Great Uncle Bill and Dee showed how love comes back around again and again and again.

I am grateful to Mom, Dad, Sam, Pete, and Pam for their constant and unconditional love. Brian and Alice are my inspiration. Corvus and Kestrel are my wonders and my hope.

This book is for all of you.

Thanks to my early readers who helped make it all make sense—Brian, Maya, Kathryn, Ellen, Laura, Marlene, Kim, Emily, and Ann. Doug taught me that prepositions are where we can find relationships. Qadri taught me that empathy is bullshit and language might be too. Sugi showed and shows me how, even when you're pissed off, you can keep trying.

Thanks to the team at Sarabande, including Kristen Renee Miller, Erin Dorney, Emma Aprile, and Katherine Webb, for their suggestions and support.

The following scientists have been particularly instrumental in helping me understand mutualisms in the natural world: Rita Clairmont, Todd Palmer, Emily Schilling, and Marlene Zuk. Sarah Gerats, Sanna Maria Häkkänen, Tamie Jovanelly, and Andrea Lynn helped me understand Arctic geology and biology. My fellow IAS/Water Council Fellows—Fayola Jacobs, Jabari Jones, Amanda Lyons, Henry McCarthy, Laurie Moberg, and

Tyler Seidel—were generous sources of new knowledge and perspectives on human relationships with water. Elizabeth Bradfield helped with fact-checking this book.

A number of artists helped me see the world differently in essential ways throughout this project. I'm grateful for ideas, visions, collaborations, and friendships with Leander Knust, Perla Krauze, Chelsea Martin, Sarah Nelson, Katie O'Meara, Taylor Ross, and Corinne Teed.

Thanks to Jennifer Gunn for including me in the IAS/Water Council group of fellows, as well as the many other connections and conversations she has facilitated. Thanks to the College of Liberal Arts at University of Minnesota for a MidCareer Faculty Research Award. Thanks to the Research and Innovation Office at University of Minnesota for an Artist-in-Residence grant. Thanks to the Arctic Circle residency program for inviting me to join their voyage. Additional thanks to the H. J. Andrews Experimental Forest and the Bakken Museum for their fellowships. Thanks to the True/False Film Fest for commissioning a poem about symbiosis that got this whole project started.

Work from this collection has previously appeared in *About Place*, *Agni*, *Bennington Review*, *Brevity*, *Cincinnati Review*, *Copper Nickel*, *DIAGRAM*, *Ecotone*, *Fugue*, *Gettysburg*, *Ilanot Review*, *Iowa Review*, *Poetry*, *Seneca Review*, *Sixth Finch*, *Southeast Review*, *Southern Indiana Review*, and *West Branch*, as well as in *Solastalgia: An Anthology of Emotion in a Disappearing World*. Thanks to the editors of these publications for supporting this project in its early forms.

Author Photo: Alice Blair

Kathryn Nuernberger is the author of the poetry collections *RUE*, *The End of Pink*, and *Rag & Bone*. She has also written the essay collections *The Witch of Eye* and *Brief Interviews with the Romantic Past*. Her awards include the James Laughlin Award from the Academy of American Poets, an NEA fellowship, and notable essays in the Best American series. Her co-authored textbook with Maya Jewell Zeller is *Advanced Poetry: A Writer's Guide and Anthology*. She teaches in the MFA program at University of Minnesota.

Sarabande Books is a nonprofit independent literary press headquartered in Louisville, Kentucky. Established in 1994 to champion poetry, fiction, and essay, we are committed to creating lasting editions that honor exceptional writing. With over two hundred titles in print, we have earned a dedicated readership and a national reputation as a publisher of diverse forms and innovative voices.